IN DUBIOUS BATTLE

IN DUBIOUS BATTLE

THE DUBLIN BOMBINGS 1972 - 1974

Dr J. Bowyer Bell

POOLBEG

Published 1996
by Poolbeg Press Ltd
123 Baldoyle Industrial Estate
Dublin 13, Ireland

A catalogue record for this book is available from the British Library.

ISBN 1 85371 279 5

Cover photograph reproduced with permission
from *Irish Independent Newspapers*
Cover design by Poolbeg Group Services Ltd
Set by Poolbeg Group Services Ltd in Stone 9.5/13.5
Printed by The Guernsey Press Ltd,
Vale, Guernsey, Channel Islands.

About the Author

J Bowyer Bell is an international expert on terrorism and a specialist in the problems of unconventional war, risk analysis and crisis management. He has been a research scholar at Harvard and MIT and at the Institute of War and Peace Studies, Columbia University. Bowyer Bell is the author of *The Secret Army, The IRA 1916-1979* and *IRA Tactics and Targets.*

For

Éamon Mac Tiománaí

Contents

Preface

Despite the best will in the world and the enthusiastic encouragement, aid and comfort of a variety of individuals, the case against all the Dublin and Monaghan bombing suspects is not proved, and against those ultimately responsible remains very vague indeed. This is almost always the way with covert operations, and the more illicit often the less credible the evidence. Nods and winks, and assumptions that shift over time, are hard to document. Certainly someone made the bombs, drove the cars, crept away to anonymity afterwards; some of these are known to the satisfaction of investigators, some are not. Who sent them and for what purpose is not as clear, and would not have been absolutely clear at the time even to those involved.

Plausible denial, required in all such operations by those who might be accused, protects all sorts who may do little positive, little patently evil.

The world of the covert is not an everyday one, especially if on a given day, as was the case in Dublin and Monaghan, innocent people died as the cumulative result. The popular desire for a single culprit, even at one remove a desire for a godfather of violence, someone to blame, someone to punish, is understandable but at odds with the reality of the covert. This is why those addicted to conspiracies are attracted to the covert, where in a wilderness of mirrors nothing is real and anything is possible.

Even those who would seek to hide any such villains, real or suspected, to deflect investigation or maintain cover, are hard to find and their acts difficult to define. Doing nothing, especially within a bureaucracy, is hardly a crime. Saying nothing, adjusting an agenda, a duty roster, is rarely a criminal act. Evil can be as banal as an unread file. And almost always in governments, democratic governments, those matters assumed secret are kept secret, hidden as a matter of national security if not self-preservation.

In the real world one does not so much cover up as look away, doze off, go by the book, take an early lunch. Operational responsibility, so real to the men who set the timers, erodes with great rapidity as the covert and illicit enters the established authority. Yet those who conceive special operations, find reason for murder, shape the slaughter from a safe distance, are the real culprits, for they did not merely follow orders. Their responsibility is not simply deniable but part of the entire ethos of control and command at the time; yet such an ethereal, analytical concept is a long way from the reality of the morgue filled with pieces of real people. For bloody crime there is a demand for real culprits, not explanations of ambiguities.

The bombs were all too real, were set by real men with actual names, set perhaps with the knowledge, sooner or later, of those charged with upholding the law. And once they were detonated, those charged with enforcing justice were unable to do so, failed to do so, for reasons as obvious and as elusive as the rationale of the bombers.

This book is about those bombs, about the acts that cannot be denied, and through them the nature of covert operations, the acts that cannot easily be described. For anyone concerned with the "Troubles", the bombs brought south in 1972, 1973 and 1974 were always a not-quite-unsolved mystery that as time passed grew less urgent. Increasingly, everyone assumed that someone knew about the bombs. There might be limited evidence, certainly little visible in the public domain. In certain circles there was rumour of evidence: evidence not to be used in print or brought into court but evidence nevertheless. Everyone, in government and out, in print and in public, blames the loyalist paramilitaries in general and the UVF in particular for the 1974 bombs. So everyone knew about the bombs, and what more was to be done?

And everyone forgot as well the Dublin bombs of November 1972 and January 1973 – incidents, not grave massacres – and forgot all those other later, smaller bombs in Dublin and the not-so-small bombs along the border. Twenty-five years of atrocities left much that was better forgotten. So the assumptions about the Dublin bombs hardened into the common wisdom, and further off, no one cared any longer.

The years passed and the new atrocities and the actual bombing operations went unexamined, each passing year making investigation more difficult. Few cared. The relatives of the victims remembered even if none remembered them; those who wrote on the Troubles included the incidents in their chronicles; those involved in one role or another kept their peace. Now and again scraps of evidence, novel rumours, bits of revelations surfaced, but nothing to engender serious reappraisal.

My notice was attracted some years ago by the suggestion of Colonel John Morgan that the 1974 bombs suggested military planning. Colonel Morgan, recently retired as Director of Intelligence of the Irish army, had, instead of growing roses or improving his golf game, become concerned with the 1974 bombs and the impact on the victims' survivors. He went on to invest an enormous amount of time in pursuit of the plain tale of events and on behalf of the victims' families. I urged him then and later to put his convictions into writing, but he was loath to do so. His had been a different profession; so I suggested that in time I might write on the bombs, building from his data as further details were forthcoming.

Morgan grew convinced, more by logic than evidence, that a case existed for British military involvement. I kept a watching brief, he kept at his private investigations, and there for a time matters rested.

Then, for his purpose, a far better prospect emerged when an interest in his conclusions was shown by Yorkshire Television. A documentary based on extensive investigation would pursue the matter to some sort of public conclusion, and in the meantime, gradually, the families' plight had attracted attention. There seemed no great need for a book once Yorkshire Television had made the case compellingly for UVF involvement and, considerably less so, for British responsibility. As many questions were unanswered as before; many were the same questions but now more pressing and just as difficult to shape a hard response to. And there were new questions, and new answers to questions not asked.

The British authorities simply denied flatly that they had been involved in 1974 and stated that any lack of co-operation with the Gardaí was a matter of perception. The members of the Irish Government denied that there had been any cover-up or acceptance of the massacre as a given and assserted that those who would so suggest – and actually no one had – were malicious. Those in the Government and the Gardaí, however, did not choose to explain why there had been such a lack of urgency and curiosity about the greatest crime in the history of the state. And the UVF took full responsibility, which had the curious effect of engendering extensive doubts about the claim. There was a feeling that many were being economical with the truth, deploying a defence against accusations easy to refute, evading with indignation the implications behind the Yorkshire programme.

The Dublin bombs of 1974 were again news, and again there were only vague answers, little connection with the other Dublin bombs, and no great grasp of special operations by the experts. There was as well only a modest understanding of the nature of the covert world that makes satisfactory answers so hard to shape. A book that would follow the television programme, a book to go on top of the work John Morgan had done, could not be a book built factual stone by factual stone. The secret world of the dirty war is not so simple or so easily explained.

To help me explain the Dublin bombs I have as usual drawn on Irish friends and acquaintances – none responsible for the result: old faithfuls, new contacts, the Yorkshire Television people by phone and others by post. The Gardaí would not help, and others could not, but there was not so much new to be learned as negative returns from those who could talk. Speculation remained the fashion, some logical and convincing, much not. Contemplation of the covert seems to bring out the conspirator in everyone. So I spent a considerable time in the lounge of Buswell's Hotel or upstairs at the Central, listening to plots and rumours of plots and receiving hints and indicators – not all time well spent but always a delight.

This is a short book about the covert world of illicit operations, about the nature of responsibility, direct and indirect, within governments that must cope with such matters. It focuses on another reality from the one sought by lawyers and journalists, sought sensibly by the everyday reader who wants all explained in the last act. In the covert world, filled with visible sound and fury, the unlisted actors without script or tenure tend to move in dubious battle. In this case they left the dead scattered in Irish streets for purposes few then could and none now can imagine: one battle better left unfought and one – despite time and the din of other violence – that has not yet been forgotten.

J B B Dublin – New York

Chapter I

At a little past eight on the evening of Friday 1 December 1972, Fine Gael's spokesman Tom O'Higgins stood on the floor of the Dáil in Leinster House detailing his party's position on the Fianna Fáil amendment to the Offences Against the State Act, 1940. This was no easy matter, since his colleagues were still meeting after four hours of wrangling to determine once more just what that position would be. O'Higgins's task was complicated by the fact that the party leader, Liam Cosgrave, along with a few other deputies, dissented from a firm majority who felt that their opposition was necessary.

The party wanted to oppose the amendment to the Offences Against the State Act. Cosgrave did not. He was for a strong stand against subversion and had repeatedly refused to accept that Fine Gael was more concerned with the civil rights issues raised by the Fianna Fáil amendment. He would not accept as final his colleagues' repeated position. And time had almost run out with no give on his part.

Nearly everyone in the Dáil recognised that the increasing provocation of the militant republican secret armies, and the prospect of the turmoil in Northern Ireland coming south, required strong action. It was simply that after what many in Fine Gael saw as years of delay, Fianna Fáil, listed on every election poster as the Republican Party, had introduced an exceptionally harsh adjustment to already extensive security legislation. This did not bother Cosgrave as much as the actions of the republican subversives – and those who would tolerate them.

During the week he had evaded accepting the majority Fine Gael decision. Voted down, he called more meetings. He would not compromise within party councils nor take much care to hide the fact. Speaking in the Dáil on the issue, he had already been so forthright on law and order that he had undermined not only his spokesman on Justice, Patrick Cooney, and the party's position on the amendment but much of his own party as well. He castigated those concerned with freedom and liberty as "communists and their fellow-travellers and soft-headed liberals always talking about repression." Obviously some of the soft-headed liberals were sitting on his own front bench.

Across the Dáil, the Fianna Fáil deputies could only watch with delight. The media had been fascinated. The connoisseurs of parliamentary politics were charmed. The Dublin political pubs were agog. The members' bar in the Dáil was filled with gossip and malice. Fine Gael seemed ready to self-destruct, and in full view.

With the Dáil vote finally due on Friday, Cosgrave had forced yet another meeting that afternoon rather than let O'Higgins detail the party's agreed criticism. The meeting dragged on, and O'Higgins, forced to his feet, had to drone on as well, speaking without instructions, a speech without content. The Dáil watched and waited for the Fine Gael deputies to return to the inevitable: damned if they did with the Government and damned if they didn't.

All this took place to the ill-concealed glee of Fianna Fáil. The Taoiseach, Jack Lynch, and his Government had manoeuvred Fianna Fáil into an ideal situation: if the opposition parties and a few Fianna Fáil dissenters voted against the amendment to the Offences Against the State Act, the Government would fall and there would be a general election. According to opinion polls, Fine Gael could lose fourteen to twenty seats, and Fianna Fáil should handily win a majority in any such election focused on national security. On the other hand, if Fine Gael caved in and accepted the amendment, there would be a lesser but still savoury victory to take to a later but nearly equally certain general election. Drinks had been taken, backs slapped, dinners bought, bets taken on the outcome.

It was a grand coup, and none knew it better than the frustrated majority of Fine Gael, trapped for hours in a committee room by their leader's obdurate commitment to coming down with the boot on the men of violence, even if the boot was fitted out for Fianna Fáil. Politics as usual, but politics amid a real crisis, one that required security legislation, threatened the stability of the state, and was not simply a fulcrum for Fianna Fáil manoeuvres. All was not quite politics as usual, a matter of the lads up from the country to watch the confusion of their enemies. Fianna Fáil and the nation had, all knew, real enemies, faced real dangers, not just general elections.

The new Irish Troubles, as all had feared, had not stayed in Northern Ireland after 1969. The violence of the confused sectarian conflict, the armed struggle of the republican movement, the use of compelling force by the security forces, the failure of compromise, could not be pent up in six counties.

There had been hopes that the worst was over with the arrival of British direct rule in March 1972. The withdrawal of the Official IRA from the armed struggle later in the spring and the July sweep of the British army's "Operation Motorman" through the Provisional IRA no-go zones in Derry and Belfast at least stabilised the level of violence. There was a new British political initiative.

It was not enough. Not only did the Provos persist but it also became clear that loyalist paramilitaries were engaged in sectarian murder. Somehow, there never really seemed to be an end to the violence, the gunmen, the riots, arson and bombs and bodies left at the end of the lane.

By 6 November the death toll had reached 650 since the loyalist pogroms in August 1969. The Provisional IRA was clearly engaged in a classic protracted guerrilla campaign that drew on old loyalties and real grievances. Calling their campaign terrorism and futile had no effect on the republican faithful – rather the reverse. The Provos had long sought just such a campaign and assumed that the road, however long, to the mystical republic was the only way into the future. Even many nationalists who cared little for the republic felt the need of IRA defenders, a secret army they could trust.

And by 1972 the loyalists had their own secret armies and

defence organisations. The majority had mobilised in all sorts of ways. No one knew if William Craig's Ulster Vanguard was a party or an army-in-waiting. Most suspected that the Ulster Defence Association had more than a public face. The more lethal but still legal Ulster Volunteer Force had undertaken blatant sectarian killings; but the mysterious Red Hand Commandos were suspected – rightly – to be no more than a creature of the security forces.

In fact many felt that at times the line between the security forces and the paramilitaries was difficult to trace. Certainly the Provisional IRA claimed that the loyalist paramilitaries were merely British proxies, misguided but deadly, who allowed the British plausible denial in their attempts to dominate the province. The British, for their part, as the year moved to a close saw the Provos as the prime challenge to order. Their leadership was not swayed by reason or open to co-option. Everyone seemed to be settling in for another year of war and tumult.

In the Republic there were many who agreed and saw the prime agency of violence as the Provisional IRA. Increasingly, Fine Gael complaints aside, Fianna Fáil had sought to monitor and then disrupt the Provisionals: their members were harassed and arrested, their arms and chemical supplies and money conduits came under increased police pressure, their policies were damned. And across the political spectrum, spokesmen reassured Northern unionists that Dublin did not advocate forced unity, that Dublin did not support the IRA.

What the Dublin establishment sought was an accommodation that might best begin by reforming southern institutions that could be viewed as sectarian. In public for the first time the establishment began to withdraw from the concept of coerced unity – unity as a right, unity that could be forced on the British and those in Ireland who would support partition – as a contradiction in terms. The assumption that the Irish state and society need make no adjustment to unionist criticisms began to go. And so too did the belief that unity would bring only joy.

Outside the Dáil, the thrust of Government policy against the Provos had been obvious. None knew better than the members of Fianna Fáil the risks of tolerating militant republican subversives. The result was a display of the new security policies outside Leinster House – new policies that were no more than a continuation of the historic Fianna Fáil opposition to any claiming more legitimate credentials than the republican party.

Yet despite the shifts on Northern Ireland and the reassessments that came on the heel of the Troubles, the manoeuvres in the Dáil indicated the old fault lines of Irish politics. Times were not that different for Fianna Fáil. There was no need to change everything or to deny the returns from confounding Fine Gael. And part of the strategy was to take the lead in the struggle against the Provos, dragging Cosgrave along behind as advocate. This policy was well under way.

On Sunday 19 November the chief of staff of the Provisional IRA, Seán Mac Stiofáin, had been arrested along with the RTE journalist Kevin O'Kelly after an interview. On 21 November, as Lynch and the British Prime Minister, Edward Heath, met in London, displaying the legitimate means for achieving Anglo-Irish Agreement, Mac Stiofáin was charged with membership of an illegal organisation. He retaliated and announced that he was on a hunger and thirst strike. If the Government did not hurry his trial, the prisoner would be dead.

On 24 November the Government dismissed the RTE Authority for permitting the O'Kelly interview: no free speech for subversives. This was an exercise in democracy, said the Taoiseach. It engendered a 48-hour RTE strike. It also introduced the increasing limitation of Sinn Féin and Provisional IRA access to the media; even, as time passed, to media coverage.

On 25 November, Mac Stiofáin, still on his hunger and thirst strike, was sentenced to six months' imprisonment for membership of the IRA. For his part in the interview, O'Kelly received three months, revoked in July 1973 on appeal. Because of the impact of his hunger and thirst strike, Mac Stiofáin was moved to the Mater Hospital in Dublin.

The republicans were outraged, and many others, fearful that Northern nationalists still needed a defender, were concerned. On 26 November there were protests and a mass demonstration against the sentence in O'Connell Street in front of the GPO. Well-known republican speakers damned the Fianna Fáil Government's betrayal. There was real concern that further protest might be more violent, more general. No-one really knew how militant latent nationalism might be – after all, the Dublin mob had already burned down the British embassy earlier in the year in protest over the Bloody Sunday killings in Derry by the British paratroopers.

Inside the Mater Hospital, where Mac Stiofáin was being held under guard, Archbishop Dermot Ryan of Dublin and his predecessor, Dr John Charles McQuaid, spoke to him. Many feared that his death on a hunger and thirst strike would surely spark general violence. Prelates of this rank do not visit just any subversive.

That night violence did come to Dublin and the Mater, but not as expected. Provisionals disguised as hospital orderlies and priests tried unsuccessfully to break Mac Stiofáin out of the hospital. Shots were fired and people injured. It was just the sort of incident that strengthened the Government's hand in dealing with subversion.

Almost overlooked in the rush of events, a bomb was detonated in Dublin. There was an explosion in a lane behind the Film Centre in O'Connell Bridge House twenty minutes before the end of the film of the evening, *The Pawnbroker*. Although the blast was deflected by two pieces of heavy equipment, the potential for atrocity had been great. There had really been no warning. Two young men had emerged running from the lane, shouted that there was a bomb, and disappeared. It was hardly much advance notice for those in the vicinity. Some began to run. Those fleeing the scene were showered with glass and stunned by the shock. Twenty-five were injured, six severely; two were still in hospital a week later.

The explosion hardly added to the pressures arising from the attempt to suppress the Provisionals. All attention outside the Dáil was on the Provos. These republicans would hold the state to ransom, claim historical justification for the gun, and quote the founders of the state to the traitors in Leinster House. There in the Dáil the pressures were controlled and vented, since few members felt that the aspirations of 1916 were in 1972 realistic or that the IRA had any right to act in the name of the people. Still, no one likes to be driven to deny the old dream or to see patriotism hijacked by those thought primitives, gunmen fanatics.

But a bomb was a bomb, not easy to ignore in Dublin and not easy to explain. Why a bomb? Set by whom? For what purpose? It was not the bomb that attracted attention, however, but the hospital escape attempt: more dramatic, more obvious. All this was not politics as usual, at least not for the Republic: gunshots in a hospital and bombs behind the cinema instead of in the film.

On the Monday morning after the escape attempt, Mac Stiofáin was flown by helicopter to the Curragh camp, where, by Tuesday 28 November, Father Seán MacManus persuaded him to give up the thirst strike and thus ease the tension in the country. No-one seemed unduly concerned to trace the Dublin bomb or speculate on its meaning. There were more protests and another meeting in Dublin, where the president of Provisional Sinn Féin, Ruairí Ó Brádaigh, along with Bernadette Devlin from the civil rights movement and member of the British parliament, spoke against the new security measures. Then everyone marched about and went home. The worst seemed to be over for the moment, and attention could be diverted to the politics inside the Dáil.

Elsewhere in the country there was no sign of moderation; in fact on the same Tuesday in Northern Ireland the IRA mounted ten attacks using newly-acquired RPG7 rockets for the first time. By the end of the day the total number of British soldiers killed in Northern Ireland during 1972 reached one hundred. The unionists continued to condemn the Dublin authorities for not taking real action.

On Sunday 26 November a six-hour gun battle took place in the Ardoyne area of Belfast, and again Brian Faulkner indicated that if Dublin action were taken the violence could quickly end. The arrest of Mac Stiofáin was a "farce" according to Jim Anderson of the UDA. These Northern events continued to cast a long shadow over Leinster House, where to some observers the fate of Fine Gael seemed a most provincial matter given the intensity of the Northern conflict. Who cared who got the credit as long as the Provisional IRA was repressed?

Now most in Fine Gael were trapped by their legitimate concerns with civil liberties; and Fianna Fáil would not compromise, and Cosgrave would not accept the party's decision, evading final commitment. Fine Gael was between the rock of principles and the prospect of one more defeat, perpetual opposition made all the more galling by Cosgrave's truculence. Sixteen years out of office in November 1972 appeared the prologue to irrelevance and permanent tenure on the opposition benches.

None in Fine Gael had wanted the third meeting that had begun at four on the afternoon of Friday 1 December. Everything should have been decided. Only eight deputies in the end voted with Cosgrave, with thirty-eight against. Six immediately switched to the majority. Cosgrave had evaded and delayed and had finally been left with only one deputy, Paddy Donegan, for support. Thus at eight that night, Fine Gael at last had a policy, and one that would appear to relegate Cosgrave to the back benches.

It was a posture that should ensure the failure of the Fianna Fáil Government's amendment and so a general election. And while that was not an attractive prospect, the party accepted it as inevitable. In fact the entire affair had seemed like politics as usual: a struggle over the future of Fine Gael, manoeuvres between the liberals and the old guard, with Cosgrave increasingly isolated and a confrontation shaped by Lynch that could only result in Fianna Fáil advantage. And at the end of the road there would be one more defeat for Fine Gael, one more cunning triumph for the real republican party, the party of government.

During the evening of 1 December, as the Fine Gael drama was played out behind closed doors, O'Higgins rambled and elaborated and awaited authorisation to oppose the amendment. His audience watched fascinated as, in front of his own empty benches, he droned on and on until just before eight, when the Fine Gael caucus ended. The message from the majority was whispered in his ear: Cosgrave's last stand was over. Fine Gael would vote no, and the amendment would fail and the country have an election.

O'Higgins stood tall and, with aplomb, adjusted his speech to finish with a flourish and so to end what had been a long and eventful day. He went over to the attack, but too late and with too little, just as Lynch had planned. The members present from all parties, the media and the concerned had watched as the drama choreographed by Fianna Fáil wound down to this, the last speech. Cosgrave sat stolid and alone, and there was no joy on the Fine Gael bench.

O'Higgins shifted his feet and continued with force and freedom and in detail. He opened an attack on Fianna Fáil for arrogance in refusing any amendments to their bill. He was in effect making the first speech of the election campaign.

Two minutes before eight o'clock there was an enormous crump, the unmistakable crunch of an explosion, and the air in the chamber reverberated. It had been the sound of a blast beyond Leinster House, outside in central Dublin. O'Higgins faltered and began again.

There was a stir throughout the Dáil. There were whispers; members popped up and sat down. Some left the chamber. Rumour and runners circulated as the watchers in the gallery scurried about to find the cause. Members left the chamber. Less than twenty minutes later, at 8:16, while O'Higgins continued uncertainly, there was a second huge explosion. Again there was a hush and a mutter, more entering and leaving, more whispers. No one listened to O'Higgins.

Then the word came. Garret FitzGerald of Fine Gael's front bench leaned over and whispered to O'Higgins that bombs had gone off in Dublin. O'Higgins stopped in mid-sentence. Suddenly from the other side of the house a Fianna Fáil deputy, Noel Davern, asked O'Higgins was he aligning himself with action which had set off two bombs in O'Connell Street? Politics as usual. Davern was told by O'Higgins not to be "a bloody ass."

Everyone began talking. In the mounting confusion a recess was declared.

Across town on the north side of the Liffey, in a room off Griffith Avenue, the seven members of the Provisional IRA Army Council were startled to hear the same reverberations. They, like the Dáil members, had no clue about the cause but, unlike the members of the Dáil, they recognised a bomb. The Army Council had met to prepare a response to the growing repression by the Fianna Fáil Government and to the amended Offences Against the State Act – if it passed. Among other measures it would allow the conviction of a person suspected of being a member of a subversive organisation if a Garda chief superintendent had reason to believe this was the case: internment on the nod of a policeman. With the arrests already under way, the IRA had to tidy up and go on the run in the Republic.

The IRA knew all too well that Fianna Fáil would seek to close them down, jail or intern real republicans in order to protect their regime. As far as the IRA was concerned, it would be Fianna Fáil policies as usual; but this really meant no significant IRA strategic change. Suppression had always been a real prospect. And there was no need to bring their armed struggle to the south or to provoke the authorities further. For a generation, IRA Army Orders had prohibited operations in the Republic. The Army Council had kept to this policy, even expecting that there would be repression as soon as Fianna Fáil felt it politically viable. The arrest of Mac Stiofáin and others had indicated that the time had come. The amended Offences Against the State Act was merely sign, not substance.

The IRA Army Council, like the Dáil, like most in Dublin who had been startled by the two huge detonations, waited on the events. Many knew the sound of explosions, but none but those close to ground zero knew what had happened. The members of the Dáil, with the Gardaí reporting in quickly, almost at once had a grim idea of just what had occurred. Soon the word was spreading throughout the country: the Troubles had come to Dublin.

From the centre of the city, the sound of crisis and confusion drifted inside the Dáil; ambulances could be heard almost at once, rumour became fact, and details began to arrive. There had been a bomb behind Clery's department store in O'Connell Street, and another at Liberty Hall on the Liffey. There were casualties. Dublin had been bombed. It was not to be politics as usual: not in 1972, perhaps not again for years.

Chapter II

The first formal notice Dublin had concerning bombs had come from the RUC in Belfast through radio control in Dublin Castle, even before the blasts. A few minutes before eight a warning had been called in to the *Newsletter* in Belfast by a man with an English accent. "I will tell you this once. Two bombs have been planted in Dublin and will explode in five minutes. One is planted in Abbey Street, beside Clery's, and the other at the Irish Transport and General Workers' building." The caller repeated nothing, and hung up.

Familiar with such warnings, the newspaper contacted the RUC communications centre at once. The RUC called the Garda Síochána. If the intent had been to give fair warning, a last-minute telephone call to a newspaper in Belfast, a hundred miles away, was hardly the proper courseof action. On the other hand, because the response to such warnings in Belfast had become conventional, the message relayed to the RUC and on to Dublin Castle may well have arrived faster than a warning telephoned in to a Dublin newspaper to a person on a desk quite unfamiliar with proper procedure, not sure who to call or what telephone number to use. This, however, was surely not in the mind of the caller, who was merely putting a warning on record; protecting the innocent was hardly a pressing priority.

The message from Belfast arrived in the Castle just before the first device detonated in Eden Quay near Liberty Hall. The Gardaí had already begun to move people out of Marlborough Street, but there was not enough time to do more than begin. Then the second car bomb went off in Sackville Place, behind O'Connell Street, at 8:16. The "warning" had warned no one, could hardly have been intended to do so.

The first bomb had been concealed in a blue Hillman Avenger

1500 with the English registration number OGX-782-K. It detonated at 7:58. There was an ear-shattering crash, and those watching saw a huge sheet of orange flame light up the quay. The blast blew out most of the windows in Liberty Hall and nearby buildings. Shop fronts were shattered and glass spread over a wide area. Somehow no one was killed in what had seemed to observers to be an enormous blast.

Even the windows across the Liffey in Burgh Quay were broken. The patrons of the upstairs lounge of the Silver Swan had seen the wall of flames shoot up across the river just before the windows shattered over them. In Eden Quay the twisted, hot wreckage of the car came to rest in a street filled with broken glass and rubble. The many injured were wandering in shock or sitting on the kerbs.

Above the screams and the sirens of the ambulances could be heard the strange rattling of the venetian blinds in the ruined windows of Liberty Hall. It formed a background drone to the chaos down on the street. Then came the second explosion behind O'Connell Street.

The bomb placed in a Ford Escort with the Northern registration 9551-VZ in Sackville Place was more deadly. Two men, both CIE bus conductors – George Bradshaw, aged thirty, a father of two children, and Thomas Duffy, aged twenty-four, a father of one child – were walking by on the pavement directly in the path of the explosion. At 8:16 they were smashed, seared in the flame, and thrown against the ruined shops. Blood was splattered on the wall opposite the twisted, smoking car. One man was thrown through a window and lay sprawled, burned and bloody, mutilated, dead, twenty feet inside the jumble of wreckage on the floor of the Brooks Thomas shop. The second man was found buried in the rubble of a garage by customers who had been drinking at Bohan's pub. They dug him out to find that his chest was torn open. He was bleeding badly, and his weak pulse had stopped by the time the ambulance had arrived.

The blackened, ruined car burned on as the glass tinkled down out of broken windows and the stench of the explosion spread over the area. The streets, like those down on the quays, were strewn with bits and pieces, and the air was thick with dust. Fifty pensioners huddling in the damaged Dublin Central Mission were badly shocked. People were strewn on the street, and those who had escaped were dazed or hysterical. No-one understood what had happened.

The final total for the two bombs was two dead – the unlucky bus conductors – and 127 injured. These were the first Dublin bomb deaths. Although a Garda superintendent had been killed defusing a bomb in Monaghan and there had been other incidents – fire bombs, shootings, bombings – these had almost all been to the North along the border. They were relatively minor matters, unlike the calculated atrocity of Friday 1 December, which so overshadowed the bomb in the cinema that few would remember it, the first Dublin bomb.

And no one knew if these bombs were just the beginning, if the Troubles had truly come to stay. The next day O'Connell Street was deserted and the Gardaí inundated with bomb scares. All had to be checked. Dublin seemed filled with suspicious men, couples with Northern accents, cars with Northern number-plates, those who acted strangely and strangers next door.

Long before the last suspicious car or man with a Northern accent had been investigated, the first tangible returns of the two bombs were seen in the Dáil. Amid the tumult, Fine Gael during the recess decided they had no choice but to back Fianna Fáil's amendment, show the men of violence that strong measures were to be taken. Cosgrave had not only won at the last minute but also, because he spoke on television soon after the bombs and appeared firm, authoritative, and reassuring, he had recouped his position. From his lonely seat waiting out the last minutes on the front bench on Friday at eight, by midnight he had emerged the hero from what had seemingly been a squalid political session of a squalid Dáil.

On the floor of the chamber Patrick Cooney announced Fine Gael's decision. "We have decided to put the nation ahead of the party." And the Offences Against the State (Amendment) Act was rushed through by four in the morning, passed by a special emergency session of the Seanad, and signed the next day by

President Éamon de Valera, the haste a symbolic gesture to show an effective response to subversive violence. By then the implications of the two car bombs were being pursued. Who had left the devices, and why? The Gardaí already had evidence to report.

Most in the Dáil would have preferred that one or other of the IRA organisations be at fault. This was improbable, if congenial: those in the Dáil understandably saw the IRA as the greatest threat to the Republic, not the sectarian loyalists operating on the fringes of the Catholic areas in Northern Ireland, and certainly not the British security forces, legitimate actors if historically unwanted. One is apt to adjust threats to perception, find the familiar a comfort. Many in the British security forces felt that of course the IRA had set the bombs, for they had the technical capacity to do so while the loyalists probably had not, even if no one could imagine just why the IRA would bomb Dublin. Still, the tendency was to look for signs of the expected, the desired, the villain preferred.

The Dublin establishment felt threatened by the IRA even if the bombs could not be traced to them, were not logically theirs. No matter, inside and outside Leinster House, both Fine Gael and Labour spokesmen condemned the IRA and those – obviously the nationalists of Fianna Fáil – who tolerated or encouraged them. Conor Cruise O'Brien later at a Labour Party meeting blamed Ireland for tolerating two IRAs, collusion with subversion, and so provoking the bombs.

However justified the accusations of the outraged, the posture was one that gave rationalisation to those most felt guilty: the loyalist paramilitaries. The Dublin reaction seemed to be that the IRA had "brought" the bombs to Dublin because they had provoked the secret armies of the loyalists. This is what the loyalists had often said: that they were merely defending against IRA attacks. And the IRA attacks originated in Dublin. Now for a change they had southern politicians admitting that Dublin had been guilty of collusion – for unionists and loyalists alike another word for co-operation if not control. Dublin was to blame, just as Dublin felt the IRA was to blame.

Everyone in Dublin and out was inclined to agree that the

actual car bombs had been planted by loyalists, whoever was to share the ultimate blame. The loyalist paramilitaries, if not especially skilful, were sufficiently brutal and ruthless for such an atrocity. The warning had been telephoned in Belfast, and the cars used for the two bombs stolen in the North. And necessity might well have made the construction of the car bombs within paramilitary capacity: they were simply car bombs, not nuclear warheads.

As expected, all the usual suspects – the political wings and their secret armies, the Ulster Volunteer Force and the Ulster Defence Association and the Official and Provisional IRA – denied responsibility immediately. Despite the denial, the loyalists remained prime suspects – provoked by the IRA. Still, the operation had an elegance hardly associated with the hard men of the Shankill or mid-Ulster, and impeccable timing.

Some, including members of the Gardaí and those focused more specifically on the incident, had doubts about the loyalists – not their enthusiasm for murder but their capacity. The timing of the bombs had been exquisite, had halted Fine Gael opposition to the amendment to the Offences Against the State Act at the last possible moment. It had the earmarks of meticulous planning, hardly the forte of the UVF or UDA. Their operations were short, simple, brutal, and often spontaneous.

Almost certainly no special operation, no matter how professionally directed, could have managed to prepare bombs to go off in the middle of O'Higgins's speech; even to prepare the bombs swiftly enough to be deployed on the day of the debate seemed beyond the capacity of the loyalists. Cars had to be acquired on schedule, explosives, detonators and timers found, routes plotted and, most important, escape assured. None of these requirements were beyond paramilitary capacity, but so far the loyalists had shown little skill in proper planning. The loyalist secret armies had not really shown great interest in bombs once the first symbolic explosions had helped remove Terence O'Neill as Stormont Prime Minister back in 1969. They had made various devices, had sought to bomb Catholic targets, but it was the huge IRA bombing campaign that attracted all the attention – some had even forgotten that the loyalists had, in effect, bombed O'Neill out of office, if with primitive devices.

This did not mean the loyalists could not have managed. Many were professional mechanics, familiar with explosives, not without wit or skills that had yet to be needed. One need hardly attend formal military explosive classes to become an adequate bomber, as the IRA had proved, if at some cost to their volunteers. Professionals are apt to overemphasise credentials and professional soldiers to undervalue the skills of the irregular. With Irish luck the loyalists could have managed. And so the Dublin bombs could be a new beginning: every atrocity had to have a beginning. But there were simpler, if more unpleasant, possibilities.

From the first there were those who had looked beyond the paramilitaries to the British army, for some time engaged in special operations, covert action, and all the dubious pursuits of the evolving dirty war in Ulster. Neil Blaney, sitting in the Dáil as an independent and intimate with militant nationalist sentiment, made no secret of his suspicions. "The whole thing was part of a British plot to discredit the IRA."

There was no doubt that the rise of the IRA had seriously complicated Irish politics. The IRA Army Council denied the legitimacy of the Republic, a legitimacy that all in power in Dublin recognised as unfortunately vulnerable. For half a century the articulated aspirations of the state had not been pursued except by recourse to oratory; the gun had given way to rhetoric. The rhetoric insisted that partition was unjust and must be ended; the British must be forced to withdraw from Ireland. The Government and the Irish people, however, gave no sign that they would sacrifice to that end, leaving such quixotic gestures to the IRA. The country stayed divided. The speeches stayed the same. The aspirations of all remained the same: some day a united Ireland when the British withdrew and the unionists accepted the logic of history.

The political establishment accepted that the barrier placed in the path of the nation in 1921 could not be removed except by a resort to coercion of some sort; and all such coercion, including physical force, was beyond the means of the state. Patriotic oratory, pub ballads, speeches and committees required no sacrifice and returned certain psychological and, for politicians, tangible benefits. No one really expected unity, except at some distant date and without any adjustment in the new Ireland, provincial, pious, still patriotic. It was an Ireland quite isolated from the events and attitudes in the lost six counties. No-one really cared about those six counties except as a symbol. Everyone in the twenty-six counties could call for unity without the expectation of having it.

And now the IRA was on the march with recourse to historic means: physical force. And their armed struggle was a serious matter. This was no low-intensity, low-visibility border campaign like the no-hope display that ended in 1962. The level of violence in Northern Ireland was simply appalling. There was no longer sufficient order to permit the law to function or the province to be governed except by military force. The IRA, for good reason, was optimistic. History seemed on their side, and the Government of the Republic was left with their mouths filled with the bitter ashes of old patriotic speeches.

The Dublin political establishment had been aware of the potential dangers of such a revitalised nationalism from the first. The effort to erode the position of the IRA and the attraction of the traditional patriots in the Republic without denying the nation was most clearly seen beginning in 1968 in the manoeuvres within Fianna Fáil, once a slightly constitutional party. During the dispute over the covert importing of arms for the defence of Northern nationalists in 1970, Jack Lynch had isolated those involved, such as the Minister for Finance, Charles Haughey, and the former Minister for Agriculture, Neil Blaney. Given too much slack, he cut them off and yet kept the party intact and opposed to such adventures. There were, in fact, only a few losses arising from the national issue. The Minister for Local Government, Kevin Boland, did resign, only to wander in the political wilderness. The rest stayed and accepted that the clichés of the past had a contemporary cost not worth paying. Lynch continued to maintain the integrity of his party and oppose, if not with enormous vigour, the pretensions of the IRA. Both Fine Gael and Labour had less trouble with the new nationalism – an Ireland looking ahead to Europe instead of back to 1916 – or in attacking IRA claims to legitimacy.

The arrogance and presumption of the Provos in particular, the danger of the turmoil moving south, the risks that even traditional oratory held, strengthened Lynch's hand. By 1972 a great many patriots in the Republic realised the cost of rhetoric and the danger of sentiment divorced from power. The cautious and the cunning as well as the principled in Fianna Fáil, in the political establishment and in the country, began to drop out of the long march across uncertain and dangerous ground towards the republic. The people, the voters seemed to understand. Times had changed.

Lynch, without seeming to shift national priorities or the inherited agenda, managed to infuse a certain reality into his party and without alienating the traditionalists. De Valera had used the dangers of provoking an invasion during the forties to close down the IRA, and now Lynch almost subliminally used the cost of an expanded Troubles to authorise a similar course against the revived IRA. The realisation that unity would mean dealing with the real people of the six counties, the truculent unionists, the violent loyalists, the suspicious nationalists, made the proposition less attractive the more closely the prospect was examined. What the IRA wanted might not be worth having, no matter the legends of the past.

Fine Gael, never a residue of sympathy for militant republican sentiments, from the first saw the IRA as subversive: gunmen, radicals beyond redemption and outside the mainstream of legitimate national interests. Any atavistic national sentiment must be ignored, not encouraged, as Fianna Fáil seemed wont to do. The more conservative made scathing comments, often public comments, on this perceived pandering to unconstitutional subversives by Fianna Fáil. The smaller Labour Party was uncertain, as always, on the national issue: some damned the men of violence while a few continued to express sympathy for republican ideals if not means. The party's spokesman on Northern Ireland, Conor Cruise O'Brien, however, was one with Fine Gael and an articulate and vocal enemy of militant republicans wherever found.

In time the more sophisticated anti-nationalists within the establishment were joined by those who would be so, who were eager to leave behind the provincial, pious patriotism of the countryside. Both opposed the Provisional IRA root and branch and were increasingly supported, publicly supported, by the entire establishment and increasing numbers of the general public.

The reality of the dirty war waged in Northern Ireland, the arrogance of the Provos, the dangers of violence in the south, concentrated minds, all sorts of minds long comfortable with the old verities. Gradually, if not in the autumn of 1972, for most in the Republic the gunmen would become more than misguided. They were "green fascists", killers without authorisation, an awful anachronism in a new Ireland moving towards Europe, prosperity, and a pluralist society. This was yet the direction of perception, not the culmination; for the IRA still had friends, Sinn Féin still operated legally and openly, radical republicans still had a constituency.

Lynch's opposition in the Dáil was inclined to criticise him not for his lack of action in the North – a failure arising from a lack of assets – but rather for his failure to contain more swiftly, more effectively IRA subversion in the Republic. In this the critics misunderstood the Taoiseach, who was always ready to close down the Provos. He simply undertook to do so on the instalment plan.

During 1971–72 repressive legislation was activated, oratory and rhetoric adjusted, and the Fianna Fáil party organisation convinced to follow Lynch's leadership, not wander with Blaney or Boland. Actually for those on the cutting edge in the Garda Síochána there was little change. Most of the Gardaí and particularly the Special Branch had always considered militant republicans a danger to the state – more so than the other great enemy, the communists, who were thin on the ground. The events in the North hardly changed the posture of the police, who had far more in common with the RUC than the IRA. If to advantage, they co-operated with the RUC on subversive matters, as had been the case in the past and in time with the British army. Whatever was wanted by those officers in mufti who said they were seconded to the RUC, the individual Gardaí gave them, and in exchange received comparable data. These British intelligence officers were briefed, were brought to Dublin, were kept informed, and in turn the British security forces gave aid and comfort to use against the common enemy.

Discretion was needed. The Irish could not be seen to be employed by the British or letting down the side. Irish pride must be kept. So there were incidents that disrupted co-operation. Matters were usually sorted out on one level or another. British soldiers crossed the border and were directed back on their way if suitably polite. British spy planes illegally overflew the Republic – first without permission and then with the private consent of Jack Lynch, finally revealed by him as policy during a press conference in Washington. Hints by those men with British accents and uncertain titles about permission to operate inside the Republic were turned aside. The Gardaí were co-operating, not about to be co-opted.

This was a posture that for some of the British was difficult to understand. They always assumed that they controlled the exchange of information, that the bearer was their man in the Gardaí. They would have been appalled to imagine that some in the Gardaí thought of them as Garda sources. And many within the British security forces were not always discreet about their needs and the place of the Irish. One arrogant officer in a sports car with the top down and his temper up could do a great deal of damage to the quiet alliance. The RUC, being Irish, seldom made such blunders.

So, as far as the Provos were concerned, the police were police, no matter which badge on their cap. The Gardaí might be more friendly – except for the Special Branch – but then so might Catholic members of the RUC. On the whole, however, for the IRA the Gardaí were an obstacle, rarely an opportunity, and almost never an ally. What the IRA recognised the British did not: the Republic was no friend of the gunmen, aligned with the Northern Ireland Office on that matter and so with London.

The British, if not the RUC, came to Ireland innocent of the ground, and often remained so when reality clashed with bias. There were those in the British security establishment and even more in London who, misreading reality, might want to coerce the Irish Government into doing what came naturally: repressing the IRA. There was a lasting tendency to blame the Troubles on the Irish, and the epicentre of the country was Dublin, so seat of the Troubles. Conservatives in particular were apt to damn Dublin without cause simply because the outburst was congenial: someone else had to be to blame. And the Irish were easy to blame, had always been to blame for the Irish problem. Since this was the case, the bombs could have been an aspect of a British misguided strategy to punish those Irish.

Blaney, a firm nationalist, was thus not alone in suspecting the British. If London was filled with those with most primitive and ill-informed views on Irish matters, so too was the British army and the intelligence establishment. It would only take a few enthusiastic and independent individuals to act on such assumptions. Even those who co-operated with the Northern security forces knew that a covert war permits loose cannons and rogue units, fanatics to act while the wise are otherwise engaged. This variety needed no wink or nod; the comfortable bias of the moment, the lure of the challenge, the play of the game might easily induce a few to the foolish. This had certainly been the case in the previous generation of imperial insurrections, from Palestine to South Arabia.

There was, in fact, accumulating public evidence that the British security establishment was deeply involved in very dubious undercover activities, and not only in Northern Ireland. In October a special unit using the Four Square Laundry in Belfast as cover had been discovered by the IRA. The IRA in the North had long insisted that there were elite British undercover groups; but the Four Square Laundry truck with its hidden compartment clearly revealed the nexus of secret surveillance in nationalist areas and, some in Belfast would say, secret active measures as well. The nationalists claimed that the Four Square people were part of a dirty tricks outfit that did not limit its activities to surveillance.

The informed insisted that not only were special units operating and special agents deployed north and south but also that the whole secret world had been institutionalised. The British were infiltrating loyalist circles, using bribery, intimidation and force to recruit informers. They were using the paramilitaries to commit violent acts for government purposes that could then be denied. And the special units committed such acts on their own, operations unauthorised higher up the chain of authority and at times unsupported by the logic of need. The attraction of the illicit and the covert for the conventional is enormous, and few at first recognise the costs that may have to be paid.

Each part of the security establishment, the army, the police, the intelligence groups, even independent formations, ran covert operations: spies, two-flag agents, moles, informers, false gangs, elite killers, authorised killers – the whole panoply of the underground. All were deployed in the name of pragmatism – the only way to the goal – and in reaction to the supposed assets of the other side. If the IRA can murder from a ditch, why are we so denied? And this aspect of security activities was not closely monitored. The Northern Ireland Office, focused on politics, tended to leave techniques and tactics of anti-insurgency to the professionals, and London cared little for Ireland, wanted only peace and quiet, not the responsibility of oversight.

From the first it had been apparent that not only the regulars, the British and the RUC, were involved in covert operations but also that both the Security Service (MI5) and the Secret Intelligence Service (MI6) operated as well. All these groups were from the first in competition and so usually at odds. Each had a different agenda, different assumptions, institutionalised prejudices, and a special constituency. Even the major parts of the intelligence machine were fragmented. One elite unit within the British army seldom trusted the other units. The RUC on the ground found that MI5 or MI6 was likely to make their life difficult rather than easy. MI6 often found MI5 as great a threat as the paramilitaries and subversives. Rivalries in London were pursued in Northern Ireland, and the ambitious in Ireland sought career roles at the expense of others within the same bureaucracy. So it had been in the very beginning in 1968, and so it was in 1972, and so it would be for a generation, only the names changing and the score adjusting while the state of the play remained much the same.

All these intelligence and special operations groups – from the SAS, deployed in the province since 1970, through the intelligence surveillance teams and communications experts down to the disinformation officers attached to the British army – were suspected, often with evidence, of all sorts of illicit dirty tricks. There was public evidence and more extensive private suspicion that some of those involved in security had few qualms about recourse to violence: so why not the Dublin bombs?

To operate against a friendly foreign government, to direct violence against civilian targets, to violate the diplomatic and policy norms of the British government, would not even be novel by 1970. That, seemingly, is what British intelligence had done first. One of the more outrageous British initiatives had taken place in the Republic earlier in 1972. Two brothers, Keith and Kenneth Littlejohn, operating with only limited control from London, had undertaken the penetration of the Official IRA. They had also agreed to carry out a series of provocative acts – armed robberies and attacks on two Garda stations in County Louth on 22 September 1972 – that would be blamed on the IRA. The operation was neither subtle nor effective. The Gardaí were not persuaded that the IRA was involved with crimes seemingly committed by aliens. The Littlejohns had no real contacts except at the fringes of the republican movement, and the Gardaí suspected this. Besides, the two had made little effort to hide their actions, as if they would be immune to any prosecution.

The Littlejohns were opportunists and petty criminals who had talked their way into the graces of British intelligence in London. It was indicative of the intelligence establishment's innocence on matters Irish that their handlers were so easily persuaded of the worth of the Littlejohns. It was also indicative of the attitudes in London that such faulty tools were given value as late as 1972 as provocateurs. Even with the British intelligence establishment still divided and traumatised by the revelations of Soviet penetration, the Littlejohn affair was ludicrous.

On 12 October the Littlejohns and Barney Mathers, who had been expelled from the Official IRA for involvement in criminal acts, seized Michael Curran, the manager of the Allied Irish Bank in Grafton Street, Dublin, in his home and held the family hostage. They took him into Dublin, opened the vault, and cleared out £67,000, a neat day's haul for the three "operatives". They ostentatiously called each other by military titles and left thousands of fingerprints. The Littlejohns were identified by fourteen members of the bank's staff. They had not seemed worried about showing their faces or hiding their accents. They abandoned Kenneth Littlejohn's car at Dublin Airport and flew off to Belfast, Glasgow and London on the way to opening their dream restaurant in Torquay with the money from Allied Irish.

Even for the mandarins of MI6 it was a bit much. The Littlejohns were not protected but were arrested at the request of the Gardaí, returned to Dublin, tried, and imprisoned. They talked, of course, at length; but they still felt they would be released, if not in London then in Dublin, if not immediately then later. And one way or another the two resurfaced over the years to draw attention to the cunning and craft of the British intelligence establishment in recruiting and deploying agents. Anyone would do for Ireland. And what they did, swiftly revealed, was offer insight into the world of British intelligence, the assumptions and agenda, the capacity and intentions of those on loose rein, freed to play in green fields.

The Littlejohns were indeed special agents of a sort, criminals turned loose in a friendly country to commit violent crimes as provocateurs. Their saga and their revelations would run on long after the Dublin bombs, but enough was known by December about the Littlejohns, about a spy ring in Dublin, about the

British operating out of the embassy and across the border. Thus many in Ireland had as first choice for the Dublin bombers of 1972 not the simple, brutal loyalist killers but operationally cunning, politically inept British special operators.

It was known that such operations were often originated by a special anti-terrorist group, some of whom had SAS training. This "Mobile Reconnaissance Force" was established by Brigadier Frank Kitson, who had anti-insurgency experience in Kenya, Malaya, Oman, and Cyprus. The MRF, based in the British army's Palace Barracks in Holywood, east Belfast, ran "converted" terrorists or "Freds". In Kenya, Kitson had developed false Mau Mau bands to deploy in the anti-insurgency campaign. Any such campaign saw the use of counter-terror, counter-intelligence, counter-agents. The British were apt to think of the loyalists in such terms: their gangs. On its own the MRF engaged in special operations, and its activities kept expanding. The Four Square Laundry affair was theirs, and the Freds of all flavours had led the unit beyond the confines of central Belfast. The MRF kept themselves to themselves and were therefore, for many looking for a British origin to the Dublin bombs, a prime suspect.

Almost from the beginning of the investigation the Gardaí saw no reason why conventional police techniques would not lead to the guilty, whoever they might be, false gangs or real gangs, IRA or loyalist paramilitaries, even the British. Whoever was responsible was guilty of a heinous crime, and few, the Gardaí assumed, would be willing to cover up for them. The Gardaí had leads and clues. They had open minds: it was a complex case but still a police investigation. The RUC had passed on the warning, had begun the trace on the cars used. If the clues led into Northern Ireland, relations with the RUC were good, always sound on subversive crime; and since the crime was so horrendous, it should be beyond politics or sectarian concerns. And so at first the Garda investigation appeared straightforward. The RUC proved co-operative. Matters moved apace.

The British and Northern authorities seemed eager to help the Gardaí and even more eager to deny any role in the explosions.

The Government was so assured by a variety of initiatives, public and private. The British Prime Minister, Edward Heath, said that the SAS was not responsible. The general public was apt to find the few and the bold of the SAS behind every special operation; but groups like the MRF had a more shadowy existence and had not been mentioned in Heath's denial.

Anyway, few reasonable people, even Irish people, could easily imagine the British government authorising the murder of innocent civilians simply to make a point, to apply pressure on the Dáil, punish or reward another society. Turning the comic-opera Littlejohns loose was an eccentric act, very British; but bombing civilians seemed another matter, even to the Irish.

Given the time of the warning and the location of the car bombs on 1 December, murder had been the intent of the operation. Whatever assumptions about British scruples, the murders seemingly had been too professional for the loyalists or at least the loyalists alone. If it were not a simple loyalist sectarian bombing, still only a few in Dublin were immediately ready to point a finger at the British. On the other hand, who else would have any sort of motive?

The RUC reported that three cars had been hired in Belfast, the two that had been used in the bombings and another apparently for the withdrawal of the involved. Joseph Fleming, aged forty, ruddy, with a heavy build and an English accent with Irish intonations, who claimed falsely to be staying at the Belgravia Hotel in Belfast, had leased one of the cars from Avis at Aldergrove Airport on Thursday 30 November, the day before the bombing. He had leased a second car at Moley's in Victoria Square, Belfast, and the same day still another car had been hired. Two or the three would end as car bombs. There was a real Fleming in Derby, England, whose driving licence had been stolen on 11 August. The Belfast Fleming, however, was not without history.

Just who was involved came to the Gardaí through information supplied from within the RUC by a Catholic Special Branch officer. He had already protested against the dirty tricks by the MRF. The RUC knew that this was a force outside the conventional chain of command and one in the name of national security not averse to evading the law that the police were charged to enforce. The information on the hired cars, the last the officer was allowed to send, indicated that the suspect had at a minimum intimate links with the MRF. After this leak the RUC, as would be its wont, showed no interest in pursuing cases into the actions of the British army.

The Belfast "Fleming" and his mystery colleague "Thompson" seemingly had connections with the British army in Belfast, had stayed at a flat near the Belgravia Hotel paid for by the army, were known to the RUC. In fact there were three suspects who had been based in a private hotel turned into flats on the Lisburn Road. As always in Belfast, trade craft had a tendency to wear thin over time, and few secrets stayed secret long. So the Gardaí had names and addresses and the suspicion that behind the drivers and bombers might lie more orthodox directors and handlers. Then the trail began to peter out. The British army was not helpful. The RUC could do no more, would do no more. The helpful officer in Belfast was mute.

The Gardaí could not operate in Northern Ireland. This meant they could not pursue matters by conventional means, nor would their colleagues in the RUC do so for them. The RUC would not attempt to query the British army. The British army cannot see any reason why the police should be permitted to root in matters and units best kept covert. They always treated the Ulster situation as war with restraints, unlike the RUC, who remained police even if armed with automatic weapons.

The Gardaí did receive information that Thompson and Fleming and two others had passed through a joint RUC-army checkpoint near Newry on the evening of 1 December. Seemingly the soldiers at the checkpoint had been expecting them. Information received, however, was not proof, although some in the Gardaí were by then convinced. Hard evidence or not, there could be no doubt that someone had thought ahead and knew the moves to make. And the bombs had gone off.

There were other indicators, facts, stories, rumours. A taxi driver had been asked to drive an anxious customer to

Enniskillen just a short time before the blast. On arrival the man waved a gun and refused to pay his fare. In August the next year at a race meeting the taxi driver saw his former customer, alerted the police, and watched the arrest of a man identified as Major Thompson. The major made his explanation and was released with excuses on 16 August 1973. He disappeared into the North, one more link lost, one more loose end in a tapestry that had frayed over the months. The Garda investigation had led nowhere, no ends were tied up.

In December 1972 all had seemed possible and all were focused on the explosions. Then, like the investigation, urgency and intensity faded. Somehow the bombings tended to disappear from the scene quickly: Masses for the dead, £610,404 claimed for compensation, and in a few weeks the country back to conventional politics and other spectaculars.

On 7 December, a week after the bombs, the country voted on the referendum to amend the 1937 Constitution: the vote to be given at eighteen instead of twenty-one and, more important, the removal of the reference to the special position of the Roman Catholic Church and the recognition of other denominations. Both changes were passed. The Republic revealed, even if in a low poll, its progressive, pluralist intentions. Unity need not be at Protestant sacrifice, diversity and progress were possible in the Republic and so in a united Ireland. People wanted cheerful news at Christmas-time, not the shadow of the car bombs. So there was cheerful news, perhaps hope yet for a stable Ireland after the most tumultuous year in the history of the state.

In the North the tinkering with the Constitution appeared to most unionists as much a farce as the "efforts" to suppress the IRA. No credence was ever given to nationalists or Catholics by the unionists. All around the province was evidence of the real direction of events, the IRA campaign: burned-out buildings, army road-blocks, riots on schedule, the country as a war zone, subversion in the streets and painted on the walls. There were 467 deaths for the year 1972 and 678 since August 1969. All this was blamed on the IRA by the unionists. And in revenge the loyalist paramilitaries killed those nearest, the local Catholics.

In the midst of the tumult and killing, two deaths, two car bombs, even in the middle of Dublin, tended to be pushed out of the news. Of course nationalists would blame the British army or the loyalist paramilitaries. And, as they had, both would deny any involvement. And so the faint trails into the North, the mystery drivers and the British army connection never came to anything concrete. Concrete or not, in Dublin the suspicion remained that the British had been involved; and so no wonder the Garda investigation was frustrated by the RUC and by the British army.

This was made no easier when the Government revealed that the British secret service had penetrated the Gardaí. On 21 December two men, Patrick Crinnion of the Garda Síochána and an Englishman often in Dublin, John Wyman of Swan Walk, Chelsea, London, were charged by the Special Criminal Court. Crinnion had access to all the files on subversives, data dear to the British. The ties of Wyman to the British embassy and to London were clear, Crinnion's importance clear. Equally obvious was the fact that the British did not trust the Irish Government to supply the necessary data. London preferred covert recruitment, with all the risks of exposure, to get their way.

The case was taken as one more example of British dirty tricks in Ireland. And a few cynics felt it indicated as well that the Irish Government was loath to reveal those dirty tricks and so alienate London, for it was there that an effective political accommodation in the North had to be devised. In any case, as yet in public, there was no indication that such tricks had been involved in the December car bombs. Privately Blaney's view had more takers – especially as the evidence from the Garda investigation was bruited about in certain circles.

Yet the atrocity continued to grow more vague as time passed. The new year brought other news. In fact the new year also brought another no-warning car bomb to Dublin. On 20 January 1973 an explosion at Sackville Place in the centre of the city killed yet another bus conductor, 25-year-old Thomas Douglas, and injured seventeen people. The car had been hijacked in the Shankill Road, Belfast, earlier in the day. Most people assumed that this time the loyalists alone were guilty, using the crowds at the Ireland v. All Blacks rugby international as cover for sectarian murder. Having the example of December before them may have inspired a penetration of Dublin. The first time is always the hardest, the idea of the operation the most difficult part. And, as before, all the paramilitaries denied complicity.

They were not believed in Dublin; but, as before, the atrocity faded from view. The bomb was at best a three-day wonder. There were no useful revelations to follow, nothing from the RUC, no hint of British involvement, no hints at all. The bomb was forgotten except by those directly involved.

Within the Gardaí the suspicion hardened that the RUC did not want to pursue matters on the December bombs, that the British authorities were content with denials, and that the British army had no intention of co-operating with a foreign police force. All of this should not really have been a surprise. The RUC knew that special units were operating, that loyalists were in the pay of the army or the intelligence agencies, that a scandal might lurk. The Northern Ireland Office had always given the army a relatively free hand in the North, but perhaps not to operate as freely as some of the units seemed to be doing.

The covert always brought out the romantic and the violent who claimed that their disguised operations were pragmatic – what was needed in irregular times. These adventures and excursions were undertaken with only the most limited authorisation. The assumption, not always wrong, was that those higher up might not want to know the gritty details.

In the case of the MRF there were many of the more orthodox military people who disliked such elite units, disliked special operations, and especially disliked covert activities associated with the civilian intelligence agencies. The British military authorities closed down the MRF in July 1973 after one last provocation, but felt constrained to continue similar activities under other rubrics – next as 14 Intelligence Company. Covert operations were too appealing to be discarded entirely, only denied or reorganised and every so often revealed for publicity purposes – the SAS displayed as heroes. No-one ever really totted up the costs in varying coin of such operations over the long haul. The appeal of pragmatism and promises of results, often results that could go in body bags, tended to convince those in authority to tolerate dirty tricks. In this the British were hardly alone, and not alone either in paying the price for such assumptions.

The December bombs, so expertly timed and so beyond conventional military operation, may have faded from public view, but the bombs continued to be of great concern to the Gardaí. They did, however, tend to put aside the single car bomb of 20 January. That bomb seemed more an echo, a loyalist display inspired by the possibilities opened up the month before. The one death had been neglected, for the explosion had not reverberated in the Dáil. And it had not been the first Dublin bomb. The November bomb had, and in turn that bomb was forgotten. It was the bigger bombs of December that mattered, more serious because the timing implied more cohesion. Yet without firm evidence the Dublin establishment could hardly take notice of the Garda suspicions.

Such official notice arising from the investigation would enormously complicate Anglo-Irish relations. If British complicity were to be raised, then any connection obviously had to be rock-solid. In any case the British had denied any complicity. The weeks passed. There were other priorities, other assignments. It gradually became clear that nothing useful could be done unless there was an unexpected break; and the break never came, only rumour, hearsay, hints, and guesses. The British army was silent. The RUC could or would do no more. The case was still open formally but closed to progress. Increasingly those assigned to the case were taken off and shifted to other duties.

Those in the Gardaí who had continued to pursue the case tended to feel that there was sufficient information available to indicate that the bombing had indeed been linked to a British special operation. They suspected that a four-man group using three cars had been deployed by those eager to nudge the Government into taking a firm stand on the IRA. Perhaps those involved had been in the British army and perhaps not, perhaps from Northern Ireland or brought in specially. No-one knew. No new evidence appeared, and none would do so.

A country filled with informers and watchers, secret armies and private nets produced nothing the police could use. In later trials in Northern Ireland where paid informers told all, no one told anything about the bombs. The Provisional IRA during their secret contacts with loyalist paramilitaries did hear from a UVF leader, Jim Hanna, that he had been involved. They had no confirmation, no great trust in Hanna, and no need to pass the statement along to the Free State police. And Hanna was soon shot dead in a car in Mansfield Street, Belfast, on 1 April 1974, and so in no position to elaborate. In fact there was really no further evidence, only rumour, and within a year not even hard rumour to elaborate. All trails into Northern Ireland faded out, as did Garda interest in Dublin.

As the investigation withered, one of the Gardaí involved leaked the existing information on the December bombs to Jim Cantwell of the *Evening Herald*. He published the "Shock new evidence on Dublin bombings" on 21 August 1973, long after interest had gone. No-one came forward to confirm or deny. There was no follow-up, and that seemed the end of the matter. Jack Lynch might tell the Irish people on television that he suspected some sort of British involvement, Blaney might be certain of that involvement, the Gardaí might have what appeared convincing details, but somehow the Dublin bombs were filed and forgotten: one more spectacular, one more horror in a year of tumult and horror.

Chapter III

For Ireland the year 1972, with Bloody Sunday, the end of Stormont, the Provos' campaign, and the 467 dead, was the most momentous in half a century. History could be seen to move, old sureties dissolved and new possibilities – many unpleasant, few imagined a year before – opened. What had happened was apparent, but *why* was a matter of perception. What matters is always what the involved, the observer, assumes to matter. The Dublin bombs did not take place simply in Dublin but on a stage set by the actors. The facts were all real enough but were given coherence and significance by the long shadow of Irish history, shaped by inarticulate assumptions. What made the bombs possible, what largely determined the policy response to the event, did not begin with the great flash of light and the echo of an explosion.

Everything in Ireland has a vague beginning. Mostly the new Troubles that had come to the Dublin streets were the immediate outgrowth of civil protest in the North. The roots might be traced by the patient to Carson or Wolfe Tone, to the grievances of the old Irish, to any touchline necessary to give weight to present concerns. History written backwards is a Celtic speciality.

With the collapse in 1969 of the civil rights campaign into the turmoil of sectarian strife came the unforeseen: an Ireland with options, an Ireland with gunmen. First, the British army arrived in the streets of Belfast and Derry after August 1969; and second, the gradual escalation of the provocations of the republican movement, organised as the competing Provisional and Official IRA, evolved into an internal war by 1971. It was a war that provoked a sectarian backlash by loyalist secret armies and an effort in London to find a political accommodation that would once more return the country to the margin of affairs.

Everyone pursued particular goals: an armed struggle, an acceptable level of violence, peace and quiet, a return to the past virtual isolation; and those in Dublin uncertain of their own aspirations watched.

In the meantime Ireland was hard news. Those on both sides of the partition border suddenly lived in interesting and dangerous times. Everyone had explanations, usually self-serving, often contradictory, rarely satisfactory to others. Northern Ireland – that artificial entity long coveted and mostly ignored by those in the Republic – was added to the international media itinerary. Anything seemed possible, and all this after fifty years of political inertia.

In the years after the Anglo-Irish Treaty of 1921 the two parts of Ireland had gone separate ways, neither especially interested in the details of the other. Both the Northern unionist majority and the southern nationalists were confident that their special perception was reality.

The nationalists in the twenty-six counties assumed that unity was natural and inevitable and would come on Dublin's terms. History and justice would in time erode the border, but in the meantime Britain should be made to withdraw, but by uncertain means. Nothing need be sacrificed. Nothing need be done but wait and on occasion complain that partition was evil and that the British should be forced to leave.

The Northern nationalists, trapped in a system that imposed institutionalised injustice, had no choice but to wait for such an eventual withdrawal. The unionists of the North spent the years making sure that partition remained a reality, that any move towards unity remain a remote eventuality, a dream of the feckless and dangerous Irish to the south. Unionist Ulster was British, and the unionists exerted absolute control through the devolved provincial government at Stormont with the support of the London government of the day. The unionists defended their own, had long abandoned their fellows in the Free State, sought only to be left alone; and largely they were.

And the British government after 1921 was united at least in wanting a permanent end to the Irish question. It was a question that few had understood in the crisis years of 1916–22 and fewer still as the years passed. No one in London felt Ireland important. For the British establishment the country was understood, if at all, through clichés, bias, and shards of ill-learnt history. Anyway, six of the counties of Ulster were British, and that sufficed for London.

Catholicism, nationalism and subversion were for most loyalists of a piece, the Republic a clear and present if distant and little-understood danger. In Dublin that republican Government, however, seemed, like those before and those after, content with words and parochial concerns. So the Northern nationalists lingered on the edge of even Irish events, denied any benefits of the new Stormont state, limited in education, property, and prospects, treated as actual or potential subversives. For fifty years little changed.

In the half-century of separation, intimacy was alien to both Irish establishments. To the other both were distant, unknown: the South a dangerous repository of Catholic values and IRA gunmen and the North a political anomaly that time would correct. And so matters had remained frozen into caricature. From London the few who were interested at all simply shaped their own caricature of an Ireland of mists and whiskey, saints and scholars and poets, a country untouched by the realities of the real world, a place for holidays and a source of jokes. By 1969 Ireland seemed far away.

As long as the politics of the country remained divided, parochial, and isolated, clichés served all. In Ireland the clichés served at election time and disguised the cost of change as well as the price of stability. In 1968, with the beginning of the civil rights campaign in the six counties, these old stabilities began to erode, to be replaced by new and often unpleasant changes. Under the surface everyone had known that violent bigotry and lethal dreams existed: from time to time IRA gunmen or sectarian killers emerged, as did those who advocated reform. In the main these could soon be ignored, but by 1969 even London was driven to notice that Ireland was news – bad news.

In the Republic no one knew quite whether the news was all

good or not. Civil liberties was a clarion call but it awoke all sorts of sleeping aspirations and fears. The emergence in 1970–71 of the two IRAs as nationalist defenders engendered in many quarters sympathy and in most understanding. Some in the Dublin establishment, even those who in the past had seen the covert IRA as a residue of old subversives, accepted the necessity of protecting Northern nationalists – our people – against their loyalist compatriots. On the other hand, some in the Republic from the first found republican gunmen anathema, undemocratic subversives who were best swiftly repressed. Nationalism did not need such defenders, and radical republicans had never found advocates in much of conservative Ireland: not from the comfortable, not from the clergy, not from those who were responsible for everyday Ireland.

Radical Sinn Féin republicans had, therefore, few friends within the Irish establishment, just as the Orange men of violence had few advocates in unionist circles. No-one was quite sure about the general public, where traditional ideas often had a long half-life. In 1969 both Ulster volunteer and IRA gunman could often count on the toleration of their own in their defensive role. It was a role that the Provos used to provoke an armed struggle and one that the loyalist gunmen used as rationalisation for the random murder of Catholics.

The violence had continued to escalate throughout 1971; the days of civil rights marches and simple riots disappeared. In response to the armed struggle, dominated by the Provisional IRA, the more militant loyalists had shaped their own paramilitaries, militias of guardians eager to defend their way of life, along with smaller killer groups that often had recourse to sectarian murder.

Largely Dublin had to stand idly by without power to affect events. At first some in the Government were fearful of a backlash if strong action were taken against the IRA. No-one knew the power of the old loyalties, which for decades had been the accustomed content of patriot oratory and party programmes. Most of the establishment, however, sought a means to enervate the IRA as soon as possible. No unionist – and increasingly there were varieties of unionist, not just the monolithic party of the past – believed this to be so. No-one in London much cared about the details of Irish politics, often seen as one tribe against another, a medley of old quarrels and quaint but contemptible killers.

The result was that perception rather than reality determined events. Those involved could see what the disinterested could not, and failed to see what appeared patent. As a result, not for the first time in Irish matters, the rules of logic, counted for less than unstated assumptions, wishful thinking, rationalisation, and recourse to prejudice. The Irish arena swirled in mists and uncertainties. This was crucial for the actors involved as they edged their way through the fog that often reflected in distorted form their imaginings.

In 1972 Dublin looked north to turmoil, open war, chaos, and an uncertain future. The IRA was not their creature, as the unionists claimed, but their avowed opponent. The six-county nationalists were somehow their responsibility, not so the other Irish, the loyalists; but the Government had no power to act, only vulnerabilities. Slow political means might transform Northern society and institutions, especially after Stormont was closed down in March 1972, but the IRA gunmen in the street sought not slow change but absolute triumph. They put all at risk. And the unionists would not compromise fast enough or with good grace. Each move towards moderation or reform strengthened the uncompromising. Some loyalists were more loyal than others, some willing to kill the traditional enemy rather than tolerate concession.

And the British government seemingly would not force the pace of concession and reform to reach an accommodation, preferring to rely on the security forces and on time to build a consensus for a new political initiative. There was in Dublin the constant but unarticulated fear that in some form the violence would spill over into the Republic; the IRA was blatant, the Orange gunmen primitive, and the British engaged in contradictory policies that brought not order and justice but the threat of protracted turmoil.

Events in Northern Ireland would not simply stay in Northern Ireland. The violence appeared on television, which brought the crisis into Kerry and Carlow and so stirred a general anguish that required responses. London could get away with lethargy, but not Dublin.

Then on Sunday 30 January 1972, in Derry, British soldiers of the Parachute Regiment shot and killed thirteen unarmed civilians engaged in an illegal civil rights protest, men really innocent of all but protesting against injustice. Bloody Sunday had an enormous emotional impact, inspired a Dublin crowd to burn down the British embassy in Merrion Square on Wednesday 2 February while the gardaí watched. Anything seemed possible. Thus, just when it appeared likely that the British would have to act politically, that the time to repress the IRA would soon arrive, Bloody Sunday put all matters on hold.

History, however, still seemed to be on the move. And then on 30 March, Stormont was prorogued. Many in Ireland again felt that the worst was over. Still the IRA, the British army and the loyalist gunmen were at work. The violence was not finished even as the talking began.

Irish attitudes during 1972 were ambivalent, whether in the Dáil or on the street corner; the old and new mixed, fears of cost eroding hope of gain. The Dublin political establishment wanted, if not a political solution, at least a political accommodation that would take the gun out of politics. The Fianna Fáil Government directed a quiet, staged repression of the Provos. As far as the real republican party was concerned, the adventure of the Arms Trial was aberration. The only valid reaction to the IRA was repression, and repression as swift and absolute as general opinion would accept. The Special Branch increasingly tightened the screws on Sinn Féin and IRA members. In March 1972, Special Criminal Courts were authorised. Stricter controls of chemicals and firearms were enforced. Close contacts with the RUC and British army along the border were maintained.

These policies went on at an accelerated pace and had led to the arrest of leading republicans, including Seán Mac Stiofáin, as well as the moves to amend the Offences Against the State Act in November. As far as the unionists were concerned, all this was farce: that was their perception, and facts, data, numbers and laws would not change it. More important, many Conservatives in London paid no attention to Dublin events, understood Fianna Fáil not at all – could not name the Taoiseach or any of the six counties, and continued in their assumptions undisturbed by Irish events. What you saw is what you acted upon, and the unionists and their British colleagues maintained their special vision.

On 21 December 1972, new directives were given to RTE to cut off IRA and Sinn Féin statements. The Gardaí continued close surveillance of Sinn Féin and IRA people. The president of Provisional Sinn Féin, Ruairí Ó Brádaigh, was arrested on 29 December and on 11 January sentenced to six months' imprisonment for membership of the IRA. He was replaced by the vice-president, Máire Drumm, who, arrested on 4 November for inciting people to join the IRA, had been sentenced on 28 November to twenty-two days' imprisonment, time she had already served. And those suspected of membership no longer had free passage. Dáithí Ó Conaill of the Army Council barely evaded the Gardaí; and on 30 December the Provo leaders from Derry, Martin McGuinness and David McCallion, were lifted from their Donegal haven. They, like Ó Brádaigh, received six-month sentences for membership of the IRA.

The Official IRA, considered not without reason Marxist-Leninist, had by late spring of 1972 given up its campaign in favour of armed retaliation and radical politics. Not the Provisional IRA, for by 1972 it had evolved into one of the world's premier revolutionary movements. Hundreds, perhaps thousands of men and women were involved, used sophisticated arms smuggled in from the United States and elsewhere, and kept up a high-intensity operational level despite the efforts of the reinforced security forces. The Provos still controlled no-go zones in Northern cities. Large nationalist area of the countryside were danger zones for the security forces. Their bombs detonating night and day, there was constant sniping and ambushing; the province was a battleground. And the unionists and many of the British continued to blame in part, in large part, Dublin.

In 1972 the Provo leaders were still heroes to many in the Republic, often still moving freely, speaking in public, meeting visitors. In fact IRA representatives had met in Dublin the former British Prime Minister, Harold Wilson. The offices of Provisional Sinn Féin in Kevin Street on Dublin's south side attracted the international media. In Belfast the Provos arranged terrorist tours and photo opportunities. In Dublin in the spring of 1972 the IRA chief of staff, Mac Stiofáin, had held a press conference in the Gresham Hotel in O'Connell Street with impunity and a full attendance.

By the end of the year matters had changed. Mac Stiofáin was imprisoned in the Curragh and the Sinn Féin offices in Kevin Street were under harassing surveillance. The Provo meeting with the Northern Ireland Secretary, Willie Whitelaw, in London had led not to British concessions but rather to Operation Motorman and the end of the no-go zones and any hope of Provo political success. Yet the IRA remained a major player and so a major concern of the Government that continued the policy of repression.

The British, both politicians and those stationed in Ulster, often felt that their security interests somehow contradicted those of the Republic. Many even in the RUC, long accustomed to co-operating with the Garda Síochána on criminal and subversive matters, still at times somehow saw the Republic as an IRA haven. Certainly IRA gunmen were safer in the South, where the population was less inclined than the loyalists to inform on them and the authorities had fewer resources for pursuing them. This, however, was the reality on the ground, not a result of Government policy.

Many in the British army knew little of Ireland, came, served, learned, and were transferred. Much was forgotten and lost, not simply the big picture but the intimacy of contacts with individuals. As a result the learning curve rose only slowly. Dublin's interests were discounted – little understood in any case. Far off in London, the politicians hoped that direct rule, which began with the end of Stormont in March 1972 – fair, just, and imposed by military force – would erode nationalist grievance. More reforms were on the way, a new assembly could be established, politics could again operate, a formula into the future could be found. Then there would be no need for the IRA as protector.

The Northern Ireland Office began the process that haltingly but inevitably would lead to a reformed devolved parliament. The British chose to believe that there should be no reason for the process to engender loyalist retaliation. Dublin, fearful of this, was only concerned that the political option would arrive too slowly and not sufficiently shaped to Northern nationalists' needs, but all the Dáil parties were deeply committed to the thrust of British policy. The British hardly noticed – it was their problem – and the unionists assumed whatever Dublin supported to be evil.

On the ground, in fact, the political process only complicated matters by arousing loyalist militancy and whetting republican appetites. Yet the security forces, emboldened by the impact of Operation Motorman, felt it quite possible to impose if not order at least a tolerable level of violence. As the year wound down, this was easier said than done, as the 1972 incident and casualty figures indicated.

In 1973 the IRA evaded the sweeps and forays, the new tactics, and began the long struggle to find means of escalating their campaign. The future boded an asymmetrical conflict between those with persistence and a dream and those with tangible assets and authorised legitimacy. Both would, if unevenly, grow more competent, more effective as the IRA sought to escalate and the British to lower the violence level – and both would be successful, and so the conflict would change, involve other players, evolve in novel directions, persist. It only gradually became clear after 1973 that the new Troubles were open-ended. In 1973 the conflict was seen as a historical aberration, not a condition that might be institutionalised.

In most ways Dublin was one with London, a fact not

recognised in Britain fully or often at all, not accepted by those who preferred the clichés of anti-insurgency or acted on the prejudices of a lifetime. Such could be found from 10 Downing Street to the Green Howards rifleman on a south Armagh hillside. They tended to see the imposition of order not as a parallel assignment but as the prime one. They had friends killed. Their government was under the gun. They, the grand and the anonymous, generally accepted that force alone might not be sufficient but were apt to focus on this as the means to hand. The political accommodation sought by those at the Northern Ireland Office and often the Cabinet in London might be Dublin's first priority, but hardly anyone British, political dove or military hawk, paid much attention to Dublin. If they did it was as the seat of Irish nationalism – and so obvious magnet for the loyalist bombers in 1972 and 1973.

In the North the more militant unionists, fearful of any accommodation that would surely endanger their traditions and consequent benefits, real and psychological, had organised in their paramilitary militia and smaller sectarian killer groups. The purpose – defending – was comforting but difficult to define. The Protestants as Protestants were not under direct IRA attack; only the security forces could best defend themselves. Thus the loyalists preyed on Catholic targets to ease their anxieties through action.

Beyond the paramilitaries most unionists stressed the need for order, favoured repression over reform; enough reforms had been introduced, so that many felt the balance had tilted to the minority. What was needed was order, not new laws, and certainly no more concessions to Catholics. Consequently the intransigence of many of the unionists made it beyond imagining, even if logical, that there existed a common cause with the Irish authorities in Dublin. What did exist for the loyalist militants was an arena where the conflict was perceived as beyond compromise, a confrontation between the loyal and their security forces and the gunmen of the IRA – and their Catholic, nationalist supporters.

Ireland remained a marginal matter in Britain, marginal to

the Conservatives, marginal to Labour. Labour might stress reform, and Conservatives security, but few in power or with prospects were attracted for long to Irish events. There were no careers to be made. Few were intimate with Irish events or attitudes. Few even cared that the loyalists were loyal.

The Northern Ireland Office was often left to cope, and in turn the army and intelligence forces were apt to be pragmatic rather than political. It was, as is often the case in irregular wars, insurrections, and liberation struggles, an opportunity for independent action. For a generation the British had been engaged in a series of colonial insurrections, small irregular wars that seemed models for Ulster. There distance and distraction encouraged independence of action, new tactics, new techniques, not all savoury, and occasionally novel and lethal gambits. These adventures were often rationalised as necessities beyond the imagining of the conventional, safe at desks or reading their daily newspaper. So there was no need to seek authority from the Northern Ireland Office or from the higher military ranks: the nettle needed to be grasped by the bold.

In Northern Ireland, as previously in the empire, it was assumed by those behind the big desks that in time doctrine, experience and common sense would rein in the more egregious special operators. Yet in Ulster the competing security institutions, the constant change in personnel and the persistence of prejudice would always have a part in the authorities' response to the challenge of the gunmen. And when the IRA campaign came to England, some other minds were concentrated on the need for an effective response to such provocation.

The one consistent factor over the entire period was London's lethargy, disturbed only by outrage, and once or twice the prospect of a political arrangement that would put the province, the whole country, back in the box. This lack of British concern often annoyed the nationalists in Ireland but gravely alarmed the unionists. They wanted a return to as much of the past as possible, as fast as possible. Some unionists, the more pragmatic, were open to co-option in some sort of narrow provincial compromise within the context of the United Kingdom; others, the more extreme, would even opt for independence rather than tolerate what they often saw as moves towards Irish unity, however vague and symbolic – giving the first inch. The militant loyalists wanted the renewed sense of power and domination that the mobilisation of the nationalist people in the province had destroyed, wanted the past that never was to be re-created.

All these attitudes and perceptions, some long-lived, created an atmosphere conducive to operations like those that had devastated the streets of Dublin. Bombs did not come from nowhere but from those with conviction. And Ireland was replete with deadly dreamers, violent defenders, passionate intensity – and in six counties an absent-minded absentee estate holder.

It was no wonder that the threatened in Dublin feared that the bombs of December and January were merely prologue. In a sense if the December bombs were the responsibility of the authorities or at least some of those in authority it was cold comfort but still comfort. The British, however foolish or brutal the Dublin bombs might have been, were reasoned, while those who defended Ulster were merely brutal, cruel, limited and dangerous and, most worrisome, apt to react to their own special reading of events by recourse to atrocity. A few men sitting in a pub could plan the bombing of a very vulnerable state. The Gardaí and Irish army could raise the stakes, but the border was porous, and if the loyalists were determined the result could be more explosions, more maimed and dead.

Dublin could insist that times had changed, that the IRA, brutal and ruthless, was not true heir to the past, that their violence in the North was not a campaign of national liberation. What Dublin said did not matter to the loyalists. The Orangemen did not believe them. Even the British security apparatus seemingly at times paid no attention. Why had London run the Littlejohns, infiltrated the Gardaí, if there was no perceived threat from the Republic? Why did Conservatives in Britain speak as if Dublin again advocated murder from a ditch?

Thus in 1973 the Dublin establishment, except for a few of the most nationalist or most radical members, accepted that the great danger of the Northern Troubles was that a sectarian war sparked by the IRA might come south. This would be a disaster for a Government with very limited capacity to affect events. There was also fear that another spectacular like Bloody Sunday might generate atavistic nationalist reactions. A wave of emotional public nationalism might lead anywhere: an attack on the state rather than the British embassy, a call for retaliation that was beyond the capacity or interests of the state. If the British must, as they must, impose order, best that it be done gently and without arrogance. The longer the violence in Northern Ireland continued the greater the strains on the Irish political fabric. In time, with luck, that fabric would become stressproof, seamless, and resistant to the pull of the old ideals.

The great difference between the avowed aspiration of the state embodied in the Constitution and what the Irish people really wanted became clear, if not always discussed, after the rise of the Provos. Ideal and reality had to be adjusted. Most in the Republic were unwilling to make sacrifices for any Irish unity that could be imagined; and increasingly there were those who felt the incorporation of the population of the six counties into one state would be undesirable. Irish opinion was changing, often changing rapidly and in public.

The nationalists in the Republic were no longer innocent of the meaning of unity. Few wanted their country filled with vindictive unionists, and some had doubts about the radicalised nationalists of the six counties. In London cliché and caricature still reigned. Those on the spot make the running. And those, like the Northern Secretary, concerned with the political option tended to let the security forces operate within wide guidelines. It was a case of letting the professionals get on with their part of the problem – except that in an unconventional conflict there are no parts, all is a muddle and a mix, so that one soldier can undo an enormous investment in statecraft.

What the Northern Ireland Office sought was to persuade moderates to stand in the middle of the road. Even a Labour

Northern Ireland Secretary like Merlyn Rees, fascinated with Ulster matters, was apt to let the security forces get on with the job. No Northern Ireland Secretary nor even his security minister tended to follow too closely those who did the jobs in the dirty war. Those in the Northern Ireland Office, then or later, who were fascinated with security matters tended towards toleration of military and intelligence priorities.

In the two years that followed the first Dublin bombs, the more changes made the more the Irish situation remained static. The British pursued a provincial accommodation that led to the Sunningdale agreement and so to a devolved Assembly at Stormont with a power-sharing Executive under Brian Faulkner, former militant unionist turned moderate. There was, to the horror of the unionists, a Council of Ireland that gave Dublin and the Northern nationalists an Irish dimension that was largely symbolic. It was this symbolic value that frightened the loyalists, who saw it not as a sop but as a sign of betrayal. Their discontent was ignored. Dublin and London were as one that all was in place, would work in time. Yet the security forces found only more anxiety, more gunmen in the streets, rather than the shift to politics that had been promised. And the loyalists threatened to take to those streets, stage a general strike, refuse to accept that the deed was done.

London, duty done, was convinced that the new power-sharing Executive and devolved Assembly would work, must work, and so link law with order. Dublin was an avid supporter of the new Assembly and an avowed opponent of the Provos. The IRA had been demonised and its role minimised by 1974: it was to be closed down as far as possible. The British had to be encouraged that the Northern Ireland Assembly must be cherished, that political accommodation was necessary. Dublin's support, however, meant little in a London with other priorities and everything to the unionists, who saw it as triumphant delight in their defeat. The Council of Ireland was merely the first inch down the slippery slope to unity. Why else would Dublin support a devolved assembly led by an Executive opposed by a majority of unionist members?

No loyalist believed that Dublin, like London, simply wanted the six counties back in the box. And whatever they believed, the security forces were daily responsible for order in the midst of continued turmoil, turmoil the unionists blamed solely on Irish national ambitions. Many of the British, individually and collectively, mistakenly but at times understandably continued to assume, along with the unionists, that the enemy was Irish: Irish republicans, Irish nationalists, the Irish state, the Irish in Britain, usually the Irish establishment and always the Provisional IRA gunmen.

This assumption seemed impervious to objective reality and remained the conviction of some even after a generation of exposure to the Troubles. After all, it was the Irish who bombed Britain and the unionists who flew the Union Jack, the Irish who tried to bomb away Margaret Thatcher at Brighton and the loyalists who cheered the Queen of England in Belfast. Ireland was troublesome because of the Irish: their Irish. And there was in many quarters no change over a generation.

Thus in December 1988 the announcement by the Attorney-General, John Murray, that the Government would refuse to extradite Patrick Ryan to Britain engendered outrage in London. This was after the Belgian government had refused a British extradition request in July, instead allowing him to fly to Ireland on 25 November, after British newspapers had tried and convicted Ryan on a variety of exotic charges, and after it became clear in Ireland at least that some of the IRA convictions in British courts had been unsound.

A Conservative member of Parliament, Michael Mates, had already demanded to know why "one of the most wanted terrorists had been set free." On 14 December in Parliament the British Attorney-General, Sir Patrick Mayhew, claimed that this Irish refusal was an insult to British juries – though it was British justice, not juries, that worried the Irish. And who cared for what worried the Irish, for had not Britain institutionalised justice while the Celts were still beyond the pale?

Mayhew, in any case, along with the Prime Minister, Margaret Thatcher, disliked the agreed procedures of extradition, preferring an arrangement that would more closely answer British security needs than Irish legal concerns. All the Anglo-Irish agreements on security matters were apt to be stillborn, because the British did not want to adjust to Irish sensibilities or in the end associate their security interests too closely with those of Dublin.

Britain was often apt to see any Irish resistance as uncalled-for truculence and rarely displayed any concern with Irish sentiments or needs: hence Thatcher's "Out, out, out" – why quibble when in the right? In time Mayhew would be Northern Ireland Secretary and Mates in turn a security minister in the Northern Ireland Office. Margaret Thatcher, of course, during most of the Troubles was the strident voice of British unionists, bête noire of the Provos, and never one for the soft word on the Irish or Irish matters. Their views simply reflected a generation of British Conservative impatience with Dublin in security matters, in many matters. And if more vocal, the Conservatives were not alone. Why could Dublin not do as London indicated, choose the simple path to justice and accommodate itself to British purpose? To do less would simply cause unnecessary trouble.

When the Dublin car bombs surfaced as an issue in 1993, the former chairman of the Conservative Party, Lord Tebbit, announced publicly that the only time the Irish would take out of their Constitution the articles that laid claim to the entire country would be "when bombs will start to blow in Dublin as they have in Belfast." Thus after a generation those in power often still suspected that the Irish Government was lax in matters of security, reluctant to repress the IRA, and generally not in accord with the imperatives of British policy. These imperatives, the British knew, arose from righteousness and were shaped by long-standing democratic traditions of democracy, justice, and fair play.

In the seventies assumptions about these imperatives had hardly been challenged in Britain, where the old attitudes, impervious to events, lingered on. British justice was just for all, even the Irish. The British army was decent and fair to everyone, even the Irish.

Most observers recognised that British society was anti-Irish – a posture perhaps understandable given the long history of conflict. The bias was the more insidious for often being denied: "all the Irish need do is be like us" is neither toleration of difference nor adjustment to others. And this reasoning was extended to the assumption, also held by the loyalists, that all the Irish, or at least all the Irish Catholics, were equally culpable for an IRA campaign, a campaign with deep historical roots, based on real grievances but with small popular support. This might and may be comforting but is based on the prevailing bias, not actuality.

Britain is hardly the only country with prejudices that deny reality nor the only country that assumes criticism malicious and ill-founded. What mattered was that British assumptions were such that a perceptual arena for operations existed. And these operations, based on such assumptions, could not be conventionally analysed. British bias did not so much determine British security policy as encourage those who sought to act on such perceived reality without recourse to authority.

This general and particular prejudice meant that in 1972, or 1974, or twenty years later in 1993, the arena was permeated with a special British perception of Irish reality that shaped decisions and agenda even as it was demonstrably inaccurate. In moments of tension and crisis the bias emerged to impose a new reality.

What matters most in an unconventional conflict is what people perceive rather than what is tangible. After twenty-five years the IRA were still for many in Britain mad-dog killers without mercy or reason. In 1974 as in 1993 they were Irish mad dogs, and so surely of their own nation, feckless, wild, dangerous. And the Government of the Irish was thus suspect.

This attitude was especially true of those in the security forces in Northern Ireland, who saw IRA gunmen disappear over the border or appear openly in the Republic at commemorations or on platforms disguised as Sinn Féin politicians. The loyalists who flew the same flag, wore their war medals on Poppy Day, drank to the Queen and hated the IRA were in this matter often seen as sound. And such sound men could be co-opted, often bought and paid for, were often accepted as volunteers or had their services purchased for a struggle against the common enemy.

Both the British security forces and the unionists of all flavours assumed, again mistakenly, that organised and popular support in the Republic for the Provos was more general and more vital to the Northern campaign than was the case. When any visible evidence indicated otherwise – election returns, security legislation, RTE policy, popular outcry – this was ignored. Their constitution claimed the whole country. Their politicians smuggled arms to the gunmen. Their people burned the British embassy. They, the Irish, must be supporting their own. Many inside and outside the country felt that Northern Ireland would not, could not have such a desperate security problem if it were not for the haven the south, for the toleration if not the complicity of the Irish people and collusion of the Government.

It was this assumption coupled with the challenge of the covert and illicit that led to independent action. Such forays were encouraged by inter-service rivalries, individual initiative, and the very nature of plausible denial, which prevented tight control on the operational level. The secrecy, the challenge of the underground war, the delight at operating on the dangerous edge encouraged the extension of special operation. The regular is often never so happy as when allowed to operate irregularly, mistakenly assuming that, coupled with all the old assets that accrue to the legitimate, he may now discard moral restraint and the rule of law and act as the terrorists do. The terrorist, in fact, desperate for legitimacy, acts irregularly only because there is no choice, no real assets, no hope but in the unconventional.

The British operators felt that special operations were needed for special conditions – how else to track the terrorist to ground than to follow his spoor? So some moved across the artificial border to do in the Republic what had often been authorised in Ulster. In fact much that was done in Ulster had by no means appropriate authorisation, because those involved knew better than to go higher and be denied freedom of action. They felt that, by implication, authorisation had been given, knew innately what actions would be tolerated or encouraged.

In a covert war there is often no chain of command but rather assumptions limited by decency and practice, not by army orders or official standards. There is consensus and implication, a glance or nod as authority, and so the deed. And so why not operate in Ireland, the haven of the gunmen; in Dublin, the epicentre of republican nationalism? It was for a few a challenge not to be denied. These tricks and ruses, covert operations, rarely illicit, became an essential aspect of security in Northern Ireland, and so seemed appropriate, even necessary, and often authorised, and became a convention in one of the major thrusts of British policy.

Thus 1974 appeared to be the culmination of the dual thrust: a power-sharing Executive in a new Assembly and trained security operations that had forced all the indicators of violence down. Various individuals and institutions gave varying weight to the two priorities – and were often seen to do so. Observers were apt to see this particular intelligence service as political or that special police unit as seized solely with operational matters.

Over the years some Northern Ireland Secretaries were more concerned with security while others focused on politics. The analysis of the position of MI5 or the new Northern Ireland Secretary's priorities was, thus, not without reality. Still, most serious operational shifts were the result of major security decisions authorised by political figures for political purpose. These decisions could be strategic, like the concept of Ulsterisation, or a mere stratagem, like the announcement of the deployment of the SAS in Armagh in 1976, six years after the unit had in fact been introduced into the province.

In 1974 many of the British involved felt that the major thrust of policy should be to ensure order so that any reformed system could work. Order was most important, even when it was too often achieved by means that ensured nationalist alienation. On the other hand, political reform tended to ensure loyalist alienation. No easy options in Ireland. Trapped between repression and concession, some in the security forces found that the fault lay not in themselves or the contradictory policies of the Northern Ireland Office but in Dublin or in the posture of their security rivals.

In a dirty war, covert, brutal, amoral, and often illegal, such divisions and discussions were applied on the spot by those with a narrow vision, pressing operational priorities, and often an enthusiasm for their novel vocation. Incidents that were the responsibility of a few on the ground could thus escalate into political disaster. A misplaced no-warning shot by a single soldier or on the command of a young inexperienced officer could have dire general effects. One harassed and frightened RUC officer could kill with a rubber bullet, and do so for the millions on television.

Often the only effective complaint came from the Irish Government, by necessity protector of the Northern nationalists. This reinforced the feeling that Dublin was in collusion with the Provos when in fact all the Government wanted was for the British security force to be more discriminating, less callous. None were more outraged by the IRA's claims than the real republican party, Fianna Fáil, whose leaders in the past had shot and killed their gunmen, executed old martyrs, and treated prisoners like animals. None were more at risk than the Irish army and especially the Special Branch, and both along the border were allied in intention and often detail with the British security forces. Logic, habit and conditions on the ground all drove Dublin towards London on converging tracks.

In effect the British after 1969 were often pushing at an open door, but a door that Dublin could not always admit to having unlocked. The British hardly noticed the disappearance of the old Irish pub patriotism. The change in Irish political priorities had become clear very early on to the politically astute; even the slow of wit might well notice the drawing power of Kevin Boland's Aontacht Éireann or Charles Haughey's determination to stay on the back benches of the party. Neither the British nor the loyalists were apt to follow Irish politics: they knew what they knew.

By 1974 the only remaining obstacle to full co-operation was the maintenance of the state's independence. Co-operation was one matter but submission another. It might be necessary to evade some of the old emotive issues like extradition, felon-setting, or informing, but the real Anglo-Irish difference was in the details, not the concept. And Anglo-Irish co-operation could not mean simply accepting all British policy as valid or any British request for extradition as without flaw.

Even the best of neighbours do not have identical interests or interchangeable assumptions. This was not always clear to the British, especially in the Thatcher era, when logic and justice were assumed to be sited in Westminster. Even the Anglo-Irish Agreement in November 1985 did not shift British attitudes and policies. Yet the difference in temperament, history and agenda could only shape co-operation, not deny it.

By 1974 there was no longer any serious clash on even such strategic matters as Irish unity. Dublin, like London, recognised the necessity for consent of the unionists to any constitutional change. At the other end of the spectrum of agreement there had always been operational co-operation with the British security forces on IRA matters. So by 1974 the Government had driven the Provisional movement underground and co-opted Official Sinn Féin, and so made the Republic an unsafe haven for those who would deploy physical force.

What had seemed to many of the British Dublin's ambivalence – actually simple political prudence – was, however, still viewed by many unionists and most of the loyalist paramilitaries in 1974 as evidence of complicity: the Republic was the seat of IRA subversion and violence. The Constitution claimed the six counties. Irish politicians would not give up that claim but only "postponed" their ambitions. The Irish Catholics, one and all, were not simply supporters of Provo ambitions but also advocates of the Provo campaign. As Catholics these Irish were nationalists, as nationalists allies of the Provos, and the Provos were the avowed enemy of the union with Britain. Any evidence to the contrary was subterfuge – deception by the deceitful in Dublin. What you see is what you act upon.

For the gunmen of the UDA or the UVF, all the enemies were one, all were appropriate targets, surrogates for the gunmen.

Very little that Dublin could do would change these assumptions about reality, and such perceptions often found sympathy within the British establishment. British visitors, politicians, editors, serving officers and transient delegations were assured of the loyalty of the unionists, the love of the Queen, the services of the past: the Somme in 1916, the medals on UDA chests, the Union Jack snapping in the wind above the houses, the kerbs in red, white, and blue. The loyalists were loyal and the others not – easy to believe under a hail of petrol bombs during a riot on the Falls Road or under IRA sniper fire in the hills of Armagh or Tyrone. The British authorities, therefore, were only somewhat more discriminating.

Often exposed to Irish reality that differed from the loyalist view, the prejudices of the club and pub, the British army and the RUC wanted aid and comfort on security matters along the border. They regularly received such co-operation from the Republic. Such assistance in matters of IRA subversion had a long history. At times security co-operation was on the highest level. In the summer of 1973 two British officers – one of them Fred Holroyd, who took notes of his adventures and later detailed his career in *War Without Honour* – were escorted down to Dublin for a full-scale tour and a meeting with Assistant Chief Superintendent Ned Garvey, among others. The two were given a tour of Irish facilities and capacities, which in any case had long been made available directly and indirectly to the British.

The British were apt to translate such co-operation into their own doctrine and their own experience, hardly recognising that the RUC and the Gardaí had fifty years of experience, differently perceived. For the British army Ireland was one more arena for insurrection, but for the police it was home. The British army thought in terms of friendly guerrillas, bought agents, control and command, rather than in a word to the wise or an exchange of photographs by the side of the road. In intelligence matters they brought the vocabulary and assumptions of their profession. They lacked empathy, felt it unnecessary.

In Monaghan the British for years assumed that they ran a Garda agent, the "Badger". This was Sergeant John McCoy, who, with thirty-three years, was the longest-serving officer at Monaghan when he retired – retired with honour and the Scott silver medal for gallantry presented in 1984. This was ten years after his first meeting with British military intelligence agents in Lurgan. He regularly met "handlers" who claimed to be seconded to the RUC from the British army but were in military intelligence and reporting to MI5.

McCoy assumed that he was doing only his duty, not a novel one, in meetings that were hardly secret within the Monaghan Garda and so within Garda guidelines. The British might see him as "Badger", their agent, but he did not feel owned, rather that he was working in tandem with law enforcement colleagues.

For all sorts of reasons such co-operation was perceived differently according to the vantage point. This is traditionally true in such matters, control being a matter of perspective and advantage always assumed by both. The British had an asset, the Irish the regular and useful exchange of information, and both a common enemy.

The British were apt to find an agent in their text, not a friend, an informer, not a colleague. Some of the British not only took the text as truth but also the countryside as battleground, assigning enemy roles as well as possible. Some of the British without experience in Irish affairs or those who relied solely on their own long-held assumptions or the manuals of anti-insurgency accepted as given a reality that was closed to the more thoughtful or better informed. This military reality was not unlike that of the loyalists in that it pandered to prejudice by constructing a world no others could see. The British security forces were apt to see a real war, and the loyalists were delighted to agree.

The result was that such British illusions and perceptions were often sufficient to instigate action. The Irish reality of the loyalist gunmen and some of the more enthusiastic security people was far more a mix of wishful thinking, historic unionist slogans or British bias, and a compulsion for action. The two perceptions fed on and reinforced each other and explained events as well. Soldiers were being killed and unionist power eroded by gunmen, by Irish gunmen – and this was the reality that none could deny.

The desperate as well as the driven felt that action was necessary, a responsibility, a matter of deployment and doctrine and opportunity. All this tended to drive the loyalists and the British army special operators into each other's path. So they moved into harm's way, each following instruction from a different map, each reading a different guidebook, one a military text for other wars and the other a potted history of a time that never existed.

It was a time that encouraged action without responsibility in an arena where many operate with only an uncertain grasp of political realities. There are always those who find a vocation within such a flux, those who find the covert, even the illicit, a challenge, an opportunity denied in the confines of their previously conventional world; and all too often these margins of conflict become not only romantically dangerous but also addictive. War, chaos and anarchy open, if briefly, careers hardly imagined in tranquillity.

Most states have at the ready organisations to deploy when such opportunities appear: intelligence assets, Special Branch detectives, elite military units. Such units tend to attract the romantic, the independent, the bold, and often the foolish, who can operate by flying the flags of pragmatism. And in time such units filter out those not suited: the short-term romantic, the solitary killers, the rash. Such units reward as well the bold and eccentric. The two categories often meld in the cauldron of unconventional conflict.

Suddenly after 1969 Ireland offered an arena not only for the eager in such units in place in London, Dublin and Belfast but also an agenda for those who could grasp a covert mission not offered, find a role at the margin, operate on the dark side of war. This was especially true of a war not declared, a conflict denied.

The underground already had a native population. The republicans of the IRA operated partly covertly and partly in plain view, as soon was the case with the loyalist paramilitaries. The dynamics of a revolutionary underground are imposed by the state, by the arena, by past experience and existing assets and opportunities. The irregulars of the state, however, although without visible banners and uniforms, still claim a legitimacy denied the gunman and the rebel. And almost from the first the British deployed such irregulars, and not even or especially to counter those already underground – in fact some of these were recruited, or intimidated into service, or purchased.

So amid the major trends and parties, the initiatives of governments, the deployment of visible soldiers and real policemen, and the introduction of tangible policies, from 1969 on Ireland was host to secret armies, secret agents, secret assets. Some of these even by 1974 were quite unknown to their nominal superiors, and some simply self-proclaimed, agents not of influence but opportunity. Turmoil always stirs the mud, encourages bottom feeders, scavengers and predators eager to act without conventional restraint. So too in Ireland of the Troubles.

Real armies, the police, even secret armies are ever alert to such volunteers in unconventional crusades. There is always a danger in those who would seek their own satisfaction rather than the professed goals of the organisation and in those who will take money for service. No group, orthodox or unconventional, wants those who dabble, those with delusions of grandeur, with criminal intent or unsavoury desires, or those who can be bought and sold; and yet every organisation, orthodox or unconventional, recognises the uses of such volunteers. Killers are often hard to find, hard to train. Those who lie and cheat and steal to effect can be an asset. Special agents with access to the hidden and those with peculiar contacts cannot easily be denied. Someone must trawl the bottom, recruit the unsavoury and pursue the dirty war, and the conventional are often ill-suited to such a career.

Thus all the major players in the Troubles had technical control of those who pursued the dirty war, control often at a considerable distance. All, the regulars and the irregular, had an unappetising asset in individuals who claimed special capacities and contacts. All had as well quite conventional assets despatched on unorthodox missions. The British army made use of the illegal and covert loyalist paramilitaries. The Gardaí and the RUC had informers on a string – often long on the string. The paramilitaries had killers on call, those who would shoot on request and some who did not even wait for such request. Some loyalist "units" were little more than the frightened associates of a local psychopath who had suddenly a rationale for murder. The IRA made use of volunteers who grew fond of the killing and those whose incompetence ensured atrocity. And a dirty war not only attracts the unclean but also often corrupts the decent, brutalises the conventional, corrupts the proper. The casualty figures show only those physically damaged. Others are more subtly maimed.

The security forces in Ireland were no different when exposed to the unconventional. Competing intelligence groups, the British MI5 and MI6, the various RUC bureaus, units within the British army, the suborned or co-opted agents of the unionists and loyalists, the volunteers from abroad or from down the lane, were employed. They were often at cross-purposes and often used for bureaucratic gain rather than security aims. The Irish establishment had no such intelligence apparatus but rather a small military group and the Special Branch of the Gardaí, focused mainly on republican subversives. Still, counting as well the agents and informers attached to those republican subversives and the myriad covert operators attached to no one in particular, the Troubles by 1974 had supplied a dirty ocean that teemed with covert fish.

In real wars such assets often weigh little, for victory is determined by the big battalions. Intelligence does matter, especially tactical intelligence, but war is mostly about killing to effect. Tactical intelligence is turned to this end; strategic intelligence is often left to those in the capital. In the Irish case many of those responsible had neither strategic vision or a desire to dabble in tactical intelligence. No one could tell Thatcher anything, and Garret FitzGerald felt no need to be briefed on unionist attitudes. The police might trace this subversive or that, seek this mad dog or that, but few in political authority in London, Belfast or Dublin.

Even the highest-grade intelligence rarely makes a crucial difference and is often discounted on its way to the top. Those in charge of wars, even small unconventional wars, only want to hear what they want to hear. Any other messenger is unwelcome. More important, in real wars special operations, however spectacular, are marginal. The commandos or rangers may be a magnet for the media, for they turn the complex into a simple, digestible tale of the few and the brave, but they are not really more than a diversion from the main battle tanks. The few and the brave rarely win big wars, any more than does special intelligence: great power effectively deployed wins great wars.

In secret wars, insurrections, rebellions and the little unconventional campaigns the weight of metal can seldom be delivered effectively, as the Americans found in Vietnam. There great power existed but was frustrated by the nature of the target. The big battalions cannot always easily destroy the elusive and illicit. Those without real assets manage on their dream, on perceptions and unconventional means – one of the reasons the orthodox find such conflicts so distasteful: nothing is what it seems, the weak persist, the strong cannot exert power, no one can tell who is winning. Even then power mostly wins over perceptions, the tangible over the dreamers. In such a struggle intelligence on attitudes and assumptions becomes as vital as tactical intelligence on names and numbers. Power must destroy all the dreamers – the usual course – or corrupt their perceptions; for in such conflicts perception is all. Every operation, any operation may have great perceptual impact; one blunder can be elaborated into a major defeat. The small may overshadow the grand in the underground world of mazes and mirrors.

In time power generally wins, but not as long as the secret army persists, and stays secret. In the meantime the orthodox find their power ineffectual. Those in authority are apt to hunger for unconventional means to victory. So in time most of them, driven by impatience, tend to deploy what are perceived as the ways of the covert, to pursue a dirty war with dirty means: lie, run provocateurs, cheat, murder, torture, intimidate the innocent, threaten the vulnerable, betray their own, and twist the law to other purpose. All this may be done while spokesmen insist there is no war. All this must be done covertly, with the innocent arrogance of those charged with corrupting ideals to protect them.

These state-sponsored unconventional means are often separated from orthodox discipline and procedures so that the nasty can be plausibly denied. A commando raid during a war is a military act, but such a raid against a friendly country used by terrorists as haven is not. If exposed, the raid must have rationale and cover, and if cover be lost, it must be plausibly denied.

The need for the unorthodox often frees those at the dangerous edges to pursue aims as well as means that may violate both norms and policy but exert a great attraction for those on the ground. Such an arrangement excuses all sorts of locally inspired aberrations as pragmatic responses to special conditions by those best informed. Such special forces, often sooner rather than later, begin to operate beyond the avowed standards of the legal authorities, who are by choice far removed from the realities of a shoot-to-kill ambush or bombed party offices. Inevitably all those so involved assume that secrecy permits all and that surely such secrecy will never be penetrated. Those despatched into the underground from a democratic state often maintain a certain innocence about their continued legitimacy and pragmatism even as they act without responsibility against common sense.

In Northern Ireland the British government had been loath to recognise that an unconventional war had evolved out of what should have been a regional political crisis. No one wanted an Irish problem. There was no rush to engage in the unconventional, but there was no self-denying ordinance either. Before March 1972 there was hope of adjusting the Northern Ireland system while imposing order. This produced contradictory goals. After March 1972 and the fall of Stormont the British authorities accepted the necessity of producing a new Northern Ireland arrangement that would allow the Cabinet time to focus attention elsewhere on more important matters. Until that could be accomplished the security forces must soldier on. Those who understood the practicalities of imposing order in unconventional conflicts, those responsible for Northern Ireland security, generally recognised the dangers of special operations, the corruption of the covert and the need not only to impose control on the unorthodox but also for the police and army to operate in tandem with a political goal.

Much of this was accomplished between the November 1972 bomb behind the cinema and the spring of 1974. The need for a political accommodation had been met, while the level of violence in the province, if not tolerable, was less than two years before. The political thrust had culminated in the new Assembly. On this rock British hopes were built. The Assembly would erode grievances, satisfy both nationalists and unionists, isolate both republican and loyalist gunmen, permit the security forces to wind down the unconventional, and allow the conflict to be Ulsterised. The Assembly had been so hard-won from irreconcilable differences and offered so much to those involved that few in authority, few in London or Dublin, wanted to doubt its uncertain future.

The rise of loyalist opposition tended to be ignored or discounted, except by those close to the scene. Ireland was, in fact, hardly worth concentration to most in Britain except for the impact of the spectacular violence, regularly displayed on the evening news. When the specialists brought the news to London, when the Northern Ireland Secretary explained the details to the Cabinet, the Irish problem still remained at best one of many. In the spring of 1974 what seemed logical in London and enormously desirable in Dublin, the functioning Assembly, was quite intolerable for the majority of Ulster. Their priorities and intentions were little understood in either London or Dublin, where hope eroded experience.

The majority of the unionists still preferred not to give an inch or at least not to compromise in any way with nationalism. They did not trust Dublin, did not really trust London, and felt betrayed by the unionists who would sit and share power with nationalists in the new Executive. During the two years following the collapse of Stormont, with the IRA campaign still engendering an unacceptable level of violence, this distaste for compromise was made manifest. The loyalists used all manner of means. The old monolithic Unionist Party had gone. The conventional denied those who would sit in a power-sharing Executive and formed a new unionist party. The fundamentalists increasingly either grouped around Ian Paisley's Democratic Unionist Party, founded in September 1971, or in a myriad of groups mobilised by fear, a sense of betrayal, and a lack of direction on the part of conventional unionist opinion.

Paisley's politics had long been the unacceptable face of unionism. Anti-Catholic, anti-nationalist, dedicated to Protestant privilege and tradition, his views now dominated a stage littered with the remains of moderates who had sought a middle road. Standing in the middle of a Northern Irish road was political death. And not only did Paisley live but beyond him in the wastelands of loyalism so did all sorts of amorphous militia members, jerry-built secret armies, new belligerent political parties, quarrelsome front groups for bias, and local defenders meeting in pubs. Many of these structures were the first attempt by the unionist working class to find means to act on events.

Mostly the new groups were fashioned by those without property or experience but strong views and historical prejudices heretofore represented by their betters. These loyalists were loyal to their own special view of history, their own bias, their own inherent superiority suddenly under threat by nationalism. From the first they had been outraged and indignant that they, a chosen people, should be denied by their betters in London. They had been marginalised not only by the hosts of Rome but also by the betrayals of the proper, who now sat in a provincial government with Ulster's historical enemies at the bidding of a distant and unsympathetic London government.

These loyalist views had not shifted an inch during the years except to grow more urgent as power slipped away to the "moderates" and so to their old enemies across town or over the hill, all outriders of the Dublin epicentre. In the years since the first Dublin bombs some of these loyalist organisations had proved effective: some could organise monster rallies or election results, others could kill on demand or raise money with a gun.

In May 1974, Belfast workers, supported by the local defenders, their friends in the countryside, and latent unionist opinion, had devised a means of imposing their will on their betters, on the other Irish and the alien London government. Since February 1974 a Labour government, always less congenial than Tory and Unionist governments, had pushed the new Assembly, and the orthodox unionist groups had found no answer. The fundamentalists had an answer, and not even a violent answer: they would make the province ungovernable and so take it back.

The militant loyalists had not got the assets available to the Provos to wage a real armed campaign. This was in fact one more factor in their list of grievances, reluctantly recognised but real: the nationalists had mobilised their masses, formed their secret army, and the loyalists had been left to their own devices. So Stormont had gone. They, the faithful, had been abandoned by the famous unionists. They could no longer depend on rituals of domination, the Orange parades, the sound of the drum, and the presence of their police.

Yet they had no desire and indeed no capacity to strike more than symbolically at those who should be allies: the other unionists and the misguided British. Those who should understand them did not. Those who should be allies were not. And attacking them would, even the most limited fundamentalist recognised, be futile: the army was still their army, the police, even without the B-Specials, was still their police. So men without reputation, education or great political exposure decided alone without guidance that a means did exist to change the intolerable.

They could use a general strike to close down Ulster until the imposed devolved Assembly or at least the Council of Ireland – the Irish component – was dismantled. Any modern state relies on a complex technological network of support systems. Without electricity few of these systems can work for long or work effectively. A general strike would not only cut off power – and this could be done gradually – but would also shut down normal life. There would be no light, no power, no petrol, no food, no water, no recourse by the others except coercion or concession. And the great advantage the loyalist workers held was that the Northern Ireland Office could not make the workers work.

On 14 May the power-sharing Executive won by forty-four to twenty-eight in an Assembly vote on the Sunningdale agreement. No matter that the majority rested on nationalist votes and guaranteed a general strike, moderates everywhere were encouraged. Loyalist threats were easy to discount: those who spoke for them had no track record, hard-voiced men speaking to media that scarcely listened.

Both Dublin and London had other matters to consider in the spring of 1974. Ulster could be left to the Northern Ireland Office under Merlyn Rees. The security forces would soon find order easier to impose now that justice had been done. And the loyalists would learn to live with the future, for they could no longer live on the past. The sensible saw ahead a season of the everyday, at last.

Chapter IV

Certainly most people in the Republic very much wanted to consider everyday matters. Ireland had too long been involved in interesting times, a long-running violent crisis that had blurred one Northern atrocity into the next, made few atrocities special any more. The establishment of a new Northern Assembly seemed to symbolise the end of what all in Ireland and in Britain still considered aberrant. There was, as in London, enormous hope invested in the new Assembly and an inclination – as in the past – to skip over loyalist opposition. The general strike declared on 14 May was thus unwelcome news, bad news as the strike seemed to spread and the power cuts began.

Rumours circulated that the loyalist defenders were intimidating those who would go to work or would stay at work. The British army seemed unable or unwilling to intervene, to do something to end intimidation. Times were anxious and the direction of events was uncertain. And as always, even a mere hundred miles from Belfast, Dublin had other matters to consider, from events in the Middle East to the national speed limit on roads reverting to sixty miles an hour. No matter how dire the news from Belfast, exams had to be taken, milk delivered, shops opened, and newspapers printed.

Friday 17 May in Dublin was special only because a bus strike had made parking difficult. Everyone had to cope. Otherwise it was a nice spring day, a Friday, the end of the week. There had even been some encouraging news. The nineteen stolen paintings from the Beit collection had been recovered in a cottage at Glandore, County Cork, and a Dr Bridget Rose Dugdale, an unusual English recruit to militant Irish nationalism, arrested.

This was good and novel news, of course; but mostly people

in the Republic had become inured to news of the Provos, the loyalists, the politicians, the bombs, inured to the Troubles. On a Friday in mid-May people in Dublin mostly went their own way, planned a usual weekend.

Soon after five the streets began to fill up with those leaving their offices early or finishing their city shopping. On the north side of the city a little earlier that afternoon two men had parked cars with Northern registration numbers. A little earlier, further north in a car park at Whitehall, several men had been noticed clumped about cars with Northern plates. In the middle of the city a man with an English accent driving a car from the North had asked for directions. Hardly a novelty: lots of Northern people came to Dublin to shop or to visit.

In Talbot Street, within twenty yards of the Lower Gardiner Street junction, a blue Ford Escort, 1385-WZ, was parked, and in Parnell Street a green Avenger, DIA-4063. They were quite unexceptional. Then at 5:27, almost simultaneously, both exploded. Huge blasts burned and twisted the vehicles, transforming the ordinary into ruin and the streets into killing grounds. There had been no warning.

Those looking in their direction saw blasts flare up in a sheet of red flames. Over both a huge black cloud of rank smoke blossomed. In seconds the explosions in the middle of the two streets filled with the teatime pedestrian traffic of a Friday afternoon had turned the ordinary into an outdoor abattoir: splattered blood, ruined bodies tangled with smashed cars, tossed into heaps of debris. Flames crackled along shop fronts and in the smashed cars. The air was filled with dust and rubble. Once the blast had ripped past there was the reek of explosives and the sound of falling glass. The Troubles had come to Dublin again.

Amid the swirling smoke and choking dust in Talbot street a man had been hurled head first into the front window of Guiney's, his body enmeshed, fused with that of a woman. The canopy of Moran's Hotel collapsed on the pedestrians standing near the corner. The street was thick with plaster, fragments of buildings, splintered boards tossed about like a maze, broken glass, piles of soft drink cases from a ruined Sláinte truck skewed across the road. The roadway was filled with wrecked cars. Windows were gone everywhere in the path of the blast, doors twisted open, bodies warped.

Those who survived saw those who had been less lucky all about them: a woman with her right leg blown off, a man decapitated, those straggling about drenched in blood, battered, burnt, wild-eyed and dazed. Father Duggan of Donnycarney and Father Anthony Maher from Seán McDermott Street were kneeling in the ruins giving the last rites to those who clearly were past any other help. There were screams and sobs, the crackle of small fires, the crunch of those walking over the wreckage and rubble. Far off through the haze and smoke could be heard the sounds of traffic and the first whoops of the ambulances.

Further north in Parnell Street, a few minutes before at 4:55, sixteen-year-old Robert Whelan, a barman in Ryan's pub on his way back to work had for no good reason noticed the green Avenger securely parked. A place in Parnell Street was hard to find any time, doubly hard to find because of the bus strike. Whelan went on into the pub. In just over half an hour the bomb in the green car detonated, almost at the same time as the device in Talbot Street.

All car bombs have a similar if somewhat unpredictable pattern. A shock wave erupted, shaped by the charge and the street. A huge, invisible, lethal moving wall of pressure accumulated rubbish and fragments, the rubbish snatched up as the wave moved outwards. The blast smashed against the façades, blew out glass, killed and maimed the unlucky before any realised what was happening. Then the dust, the floating paper, the bits of rubble began to drift down into the street. It was quiet for a moment, with only the tinkle of falling glass to be heard before the screaming began. The explosion blew in the front of buildings along Parnell Street, turned unlucky pedestrians into victims, and shocked and stunned the others. It was so quick, so deadly, so unexpected that few understood what had happened.

The blast killed five outright. A woman with a baby in a pram were hit, tossed in the air. The baby disappeared within one of the shattered shop windows. Dominick O'Shea, the manager of the Welcome Inn, and his patrons rushed out and scrambled after it. There amid the rubble they found the baby, alive and untouched in the basement atop the collapsed shop front.

Not all were as lucky. A ruined body, an eye gone, the face torn open, was found. Two men were thrown through the front windows of a garage, mangled and dead even before the rubble buried them. They remained for a time on the edge of events, two warped, bloody heaps hidden just inside on the floor.

In a second the bomb car was a twisted, burnt-black frame at the centre of the destruction. What remained was hardly recognisable as a car. The hot hulk lay under a pall of black smoke, dust and bits of paper floating in the hot air above the street. It had been reduced to a small core, the engine block, the main frame and axles distorted, a strange artefact of modern violence. About it drifted only a few burning bits and the sharp smell of cordite. Its presence told survivors what had happened. They stood amid an instant ruin.

The row of parking meters in Parnell Street stuck up through the tide of rubble, markers in a maze of broken boards, spilt plaster, glass, the hulks of cars ruined and cars tossed like unwanted toys into the street. One body lay torn and bleeding beside the wheel of a smashed car. One man had a leg missing, another the side of his head. A child of twelve lay in the gutter. A man lay motionless by a dirty and dented Fiat car. The men from the Welcome Inn were digging for the baby; others standing covered in dust did not know where to begin, what to do.

It was difficult to tell who was alive. The street was heaped in bits thrown from the smashed buildings, the rubble often splattered with blood. Antonio Magliocci was dead in his demolished fish-and-chip shop. Someone covered a man's body with newspapers. For a long time, as the search for the living and aid for the injured absorbed everyone, he lay under his newspapers, a dreadful, still memorial to murder.

Further down in Marlborough Street the seven-storey head office of the Department of Posts and Telegraphs had lost its windows; the staff on the way out had been sprayed with glass. Slivers of glass driven horizontally by the explosion cut a deadly path through anything as soft and fragile as people, sliced, skewered, hacked, almost before the sound could reach them.

The ambulances began to arrive. The Dublin Red Alert, established six years before by the Garda Síochána, the Fire Service and the Irish Medical Association, meant a swift emergency response and a shuttle to the nearest city hospitals. Firefighters appeared, dressed for disaster, to find little burning, just smudges, embers, and the hot, twisted metal of the blasted cars. They joined the gardaí in trying to help.

Some victims were obviously beyond all help. Esma Crabbe, only fifteen but a member of the St John Ambulance Brigade, took the pulse of the man by the Fiat. Too late for him. She moved on while others, still shocked, not yet come to terms with disaster, stood about waiting. Father Bernard McGuckian from Gardiner Street church knelt in the ashes on the street and anointed five. Father John Killeen from the church in Berkeley Road anointed five more, one a baby girl. "It was diabolical," he said. Certainly the scene smelt of sulphur and flames.

Further along a man of about fifty, neatly dressed in suit and striped shirt, dark tie, and polished shoes, stood, hands in his pockets, eyes unfocused, waiting for instructions, waiting for explanation. There was no explanation. Hardly anyone north of the Liffey near the bomb sites could think of anything but the immediate horror, the slaughter, the smashed, the carnage. Enough for the moment that two bombs had done the damage.

Across the Liffey on the south side of the city a few minutes later, at 5:33 p.m., with a third bright-red flash and a third horrendous roar, an estimated twenty pounds of high explosive detonated in a green Austin 1800, registration number HOI-2487. This car had been parked in South Leinster Street, seventy-five yards from the junction of Lincoln Place and so not far from the Dáil and Government Buildings. It had been parked, locked and left only ten minutes before the explosion, only a nervous margin before the timer turned over, and only minutes after the first device went off in Talbot Street. The driver had obviously had problems in finding a parking place.

In South Leinster Street no one knew of the catastrophe across town. Only a few had even registered the distant thud of the explosions. The blast and flash had come totally without warning, swept down the street, wiped away the normal. All those in or near the street were dazed and shattered by the enormous explosion, tossed about, thrown from their chairs or into the roadway. A man and a young woman were killed instantly. The woman had passed between the bomb car and the Trinity College wall opposite Neenan's travel agency at the very moment of detonation. Her body lay on the street burning in the swirling smoke. Beside her, almost neatly amid the rubble and ash, were her mauve shoes, side by side, untouched. Garda Fitzgerald rushed towards her, took off his coat and tried to douse the flames. Instead of newspapers she had a police coat as shroud. The other victim lay smouldering in the street, clearly dead. He had been too close to the car bomb, never knew what had happened. One minute a pedestrian rushing about on a Friday afternoon, the next a burnt ember.

Michael Duffy and his wife, sitting in their parked car fifty yards from the blast, had the front windscreen come to pieces in their faces yet with hardly any damage. An elderly man standing closer to the blast had both legs smashed, a foot blown off. At least a dozen of the injured were scattered along the street, blackened, burned, bleeding, dazed and moaning. Some stood, some sat, a few staggered about.

The nearby offices were shattered: Chubb Alarms, Phoenix Assurance, Bowmakers Finance, and the Cherry Tree restaurant. One minute everyone stirring about at the end of the day, then the roar, the hot flash, and the glass sprayed over everyone. Once the echo of the bomb was over, the moment of silence passed and everyone could hear the clatter and tinkle of falling debris, shattered glass, bits of the car. Many of those who escaped began to scream, in terror or in pain.

Thomas McKeever had been blown out of his chair in the Cherry Tree restaurant. He got to his feet amid the ruins and reached the door to see Garda Fitzgerald beating at the body of a burning woman. Once the fire was out, the coat draped, he, like McKeever, looked about to see what else could be done. Others began to stumble out into South Leinster Street.

Some, as at the other bomb sites, were simply dazed, made no effort to move, to escape, to help anyone, stood still, shocked. A few took charge, helped the shattered. Four Chubb employees standing near the windows on the second floor had been showered with glass, then along with those from the other offices came into the street to help the injured. Another man, impatient for the ambulances, drove two people to hospital through the stalled traffic and uncertain crowds. The old man with his foot blown off, all his clothes still smouldering, writhed in pain. The dead man lay motionless, a leg gone, one side of his head completely ripped away.

A twelve-year-old lay nearby, whimpering. There was blood all over the place. A girl in severe pain was brought into Chubb Alarms. Her hair was singed, her clothes burnt or torn off, her legs slashed and gashed. In less than fifteen minutes the ambulances began to arrive. It had seemed to those on the ground to have taken for ever. Time stops for the blast and the fall of the glass and then creeps as the maimed lie unattended even when help is almost instant.

The Dublin Red Alert did get help to the damaged quickly and the injured to the waiting emergency rooms. Extra staff were on their way into the hospitals. Blood donors were already in line. All the while the ambulances moved out the injured, the crush barriers went up, the shocked and uncertain wandered off towards home.

They left behind a street strewn with glass, smouldering debris and the twisted, blackened ruin of the bomb car, a compressed black device, the engine at the centre, one wheel visible and the rest a snarl of stressed and smoking metal. The crowds at the ends of the street thinned. The smell of explosion and burnt debris faded. The mauve shoes and the young woman's body were gone at last. She had become one more fatality, another number along with her unknown dead companion on the littered street, both soon entries in the books of the City Morgue across the river, where staff began receiving almost as soon as the hospitals.

The hospitals worked overtime to cope with the damaged and dying. Within forty minutes the last of the victims were off the streets and in the emergency rooms. The death toll was still being totted up and correlated by the authorities: fifteen women, six men, two baby girls, perhaps more, certainly more. For those who lived there were horrible injuries to treat. Preparations were being made at the morgue to receive those who had died of damages from blast: crushed tissue, massive, uncontrollable haemorrhages and multiple internal injuries, destroyed organs, shock.

Not all who had escaped death would escape for long. Some would be scarred for life, maimed, limbs gone, lives transformed in seconds. And beyond the immediate pain and blood and burnt flesh would come the other losses: the father dead, the whole family gone, the child to live as a cripple, the wife to miscarry. Some would never forget, could never forget the white-hot flash, the sick moment of pain, for the rest of their lives would remember the panic and be able to touch the scar.

There were new widows and new orphans still asleep in their beds. A sick woman could not be told of her loss. Others in the country would not learn about their losses until later that evening, a daughter dead in Dublin while shopping or a cousin lost for ever. All that was for later.

And no one knew what else to expect: more bombs, more innocent people ruined for no purpose? The Gardaí announced that the three explosions might not be the end of such attacks. Already the fear of more had spread. In the city the first false alarms and telephoned suspicions began flooding the switchboards. A couple from Armagh were picked up and kept in the Bridewell until in the light of the next day they were found innocent. Suspicious cars had been seen, driving the wrong way or too slowly or simply parked on an expired meter. Strange men had asked for directions. People with Northern accents were questioned, reported, avoided. Again and again on Friday evening and over the weekend, car bombs were suspected here or there.

Beyond Dublin the country began to learn of its worst crime, the greatest number ever killed at once, the most violent moment of the entire Troubles – and the day not over. The radio began broadcasting Bach cello music and reports of the tragedy. A pall of anxiety but not yet anger settled on the capital.

In Monaghan town, after the Dublin bombs but not in time for anyone to respond – and what could be done in any case? – the last act of the tragedy occurred just over an hour later. At 6:42 p.m. a green Hillman Minx exploded. It had been stolen from a car park in Portadown between half past five and six earlier that day and driven into Monaghan at teatime. A back-up car, also stolen, had trailed it all the way, waiting to rush the driver back across the border. The Hillman had finally been hastily parked outside Greacon's Pub in Church Street by a man denied a space further up the street. Greacon's café was well known to many beyond Monaghan as the express bus stop.

The explosion all but demolished Greacon's. The front was smashed, slates torn off the roof, the whole building warped by the blast. The windows all up and down the street were shattered. The area was filled with thick smoke and the tell-tale smell of cordite.

Jack Travers, aged twenty-nine, a lorry driver due to be married in July, was sitting in his car in Church Street when the blast wave killed him before he even sensed danger. The shock wave that smashed in the wooden walls of Greacon's, scattering the planks, dropping the sign to street level and producing a twisting cloud of smoke, also blew much of the café front into the street. There two cars burned in the wreckage. Across the street the windows and doors of the Hibernian Bank were gone, the roof unsupported.

For two hundred yards along Church Street the windows were gone. Inside the café the blast had torn into the first floor and killed Peggy White, manager of the pub, a woman in her early forties with a family. Altogether five were dead, one not immediately identified, and twenty-eight injured.

The next day the screaming headlines indicated the first butcher's bill, losses that would ultimately reach thirty-three dead and over three hundred injured. At Talbot Street John O'Brien, aged twenty-three, of Lower Gardiner Street, his wife, Anne O'Brien, aged twenty-two, and their two daughters, aged seventeen months and five months, were dead. A thirty-year-old French woman, Simone Chetrix, who had been in Dublin as an au pair, was due to return to Paris on Sunday; forty-eight hours left and time to shop in Talbot Street, to pass by the blue Ford Escort at half five.

There were people from out of town like Marie Butley from Cappoquin, County Waterford, and all the others: Colette O'Doherty, aged twenty-one, of Sheriff Street in Dublin; George Williamson, an elderly farmer from Castlehoe, outside Monaghan, people without fame, largely people of no property, everyday people on their way elsewhere. And instead of being here or there, home or out for a drink, on the evening of 17 May just past teatime they were in a morgue, tagged, their names on the lists handed to the fearful families and waiting journalists.

At the end there were to be thirty-three names, and a Requiem Mass in the Pro-Cathedral for twelve of the victims attended by the Taoiseach and the President. The others had services in Dublin, Monaghan, and the country churches: a funereal week.

For many that day would define their life, their luck. They had been here or there just too early, stayed a moment, left a minute too soon. Seán Ó Brádaigh, director of publicity for Provisional Sinn Féin, had just walked by one of the car bombs on the north side. Conor Cruise O'Brien's daughter Kate Cruise O'Brien had come out of the Nassau Street entrance of Trinity College just a minute too soon for the bomb. Many would remember where they were that Friday afternoon; and too many would remember only that it was the last normal day before someone, for some reason, cut into their lives for uncertain purpose.

Before the last of the injured had reached hospital the Gardaí were at work, all resources focused on finding just who had been responsible. They soon had special teams seeking the culprits. Everyone from the first, not without reason, suspected loyalists: who else would murder innocent people merely because they were on the streets of Dublin? In the midst of a general strike, a confrontation with their unfaithful ally the British, who else but the loyalists would vent their frustration on those in Dublin guilty of nothing but their nationality?

The Minister for Justice, Patrick Cooney, could already announce that two of the cars used in Dublin had been stolen from loyalist areas of Belfast. At ten on Friday night, with the tang of cordite still in the air, Liam Cosgrave, head of the Coalition Government since the unexpected defeat of Fianna Fáil in February, spoke to a stunned nation on television. He spoke with revulsion, condemnation for the unknown bombers and all who would undertake such "criminal folly" – an "unforgivable act." He damned the "utter futility of violent action as a means for furthering political ends." Clearly he had the IRA in mind as much as the suspected loyalists. "Everyone who has practised violence or preached violence or condoned violence must bear a share of responsibility for today's outrage." He said that the bomb would help "to bring home to us here what the people in Northern Ireland have been suffering for five long years." The deaths were a direct result of those who had introduced the gun into politics: the private killers, the secret armies, the vigilantes and defenders, the Provos.

Cosgrave, like many, would see the tragedy shaped by a special perspective, learn lessons already known, preach to the converted amid the horror. The fault lay not so much with the loyalists as with the republican movement, the clear and present danger. Unwittingly Cosgrave and the others simply stressed the reason behind the unreasoning loyalist bombs: if we are threatened by the IRA, so too shall you be. This was why the bombs were set: to assuage loyalist anxiety, not to impose political change, not to a strategic timetable.

Others in the Republic focused not on the provocation of the IRA but on those who set the bombs. What could they gain? Why had they come to Dublin? Was this a beginning or an aberration? Anxiety that took the form of atrocity was difficult to grasp, even in Dublin, even after exposure to the Troubles. The Government had as yet no answers, only anxiety and repulsion. And repulsion is a momentary emotion.

For those not directly touched, the horror would begin to fade as the threat of more bombs diminished and the rituals of passage ended. And then there would be nothing for the others, the survivors, those damaged by the blast, those with ruined lives, those physically untouched but bereaved: nothing but to adjust.

The loyalist paramilitaries denied any part in the Dublin bombs. The loyalists, the unionists, many in Britain and Northern Ireland without local politics assumed, whatever the paramilitary spokesmen might say, that Cosgrave was right. The bombs had come to Dublin as retaliation for IRA provocation – timed to go with the general strike. Many or most believed the bombs went off to bring the war to the Republic, to reveal the cost of collusion, to force Dublin to close down the IRA. No wonder the UDA press officer, Sammy Smyth, always a man for the hard word, in the midst of the turmoil caused by the general strike still found time to tell the media that "I am very happy about the bombings in Dublin. There is a war with the Free State, and now we are laughing at them."

No one else had the audacity to laugh. Those who would have done so, the unrepentant loyalists, kept still. The rest in Ireland and elsewhere were appalled. The Pope in Rome, noting that only God had the right to take life, sent his condolences in a telegram to the Archbishop of Dublin, called it a week of blood, condemned "these acts as unworthy of human conduct," and urged everyone to restore harmony and peace. Everyone near and far condemned the bombs. No one claimed the deed. All the paramilitaries – including Sammy Smyth's UDA – continued to deny responsibility. The "Ulster Loyalist Front", spokesmen for the UVF, condemned the bombing without reservation. The Provisional IRA called it a "vile murder".

The Northern Ireland Chief Executive, Brian Faulkner, under siege from the loyalist workers' strike, sent a message to Liam

Cosgrave expressing "deepest regret . . . Whatever the differences of opinion which may exist in other matters, I believe the responsible people in Northern Ireland and the Republic alike want to see this island rid for ever of the evil forces which are guilty of such acts." In London the British establishment followed suit. The conservative *Sunday Telegraph* felt that the bombs "are the work of evil men who deserved not only reprobation but also punishment far more severe than that which weak-minded liberal communities are willing to inflict."

No one – except those who blamed IRA provocation – had a reasoned explanation for the bombs. The thirty-three victims seemed to have died as a result of malice, a vile act of spite, loathsome murder without justification. And yet skill and cunning, reasoned planning and a sense of purpose had been necessary to shape the entire operation.

Chapter V

The Dublin bombs seemed pointless, to have little apparent impact on events. In Northern Ireland those advocates of the new power-sharing Executive continued to focus on the general strike and the seeming failure of the security forces, in particular the British army commanders, to take strong action against intimidation. The Northern Ireland Office appeared unwilling to intervene to effect in the strike, end intimidation, or act on behalf of the new and still fragile Assembly. Increasingly the general strike appeared beyond the capacities of the Northern Ireland Secretary, Merlyn Rees, or the British army to break. No Dublin bombs seemed needed.

Those in responsibility in Belfast and London claimed that the British army could not make the workers work nor turn back events, nor run the power stations; could not guarantee petrol supplies or keep the province working. And normal life in the province was demonstrably winding down.

The loyalists seemed to be winning, without bombs, and Dublin watched in dismay as the British talked on with the loyalist organisations that all in the Republic were convinced had instigated the Dublin and Monaghan bombs. And those bombs, so unexpected, so lethal, seemed so pointless, at best merely emphasising the known predilections and prejudices of the loyalists and at worst random murder by brutal, ruthless and stupid men. Yet, stupid or no, the bombing operation had been a "success": all the cars detonated seemingly on schedule and all those involved were away clear; someone had thought the exercise worth the trouble.

Yet the Troubles continued as before. The IRA went their way unrepentant, no more and no less willing to be charged with provocation. On Saturday 18 May bombs exploded in two postboxes in Lisburn and seriously injured an RUC man and thirty-two others. There was an IRA bomb in a jeweller's shop in Lurgan, a loyalist bomb at a pub in Skegoneill Avenue, shots fired, incidents reported, and an arms find at the Twinbrook estate in Belfast. The next day another car bomb exploded, this time in the multi-storey car park at Heathrow Airport, London, damaging fifty cars and slightly injuring two people.

Even amid the noise of the IRA campaign – always louder with English incidents – and with the loyalist strike drama threatening to overturn the whole Sunningdale accommodation, the fallout of the Dublin bombs remained hard news. The international media always hovered in London waiting for an Irish atrocity or a novel spectacular. Bombs in Dublin fitted the bill: thirty-three dead, the most lethal one-day total to date for the Troubles.

The resources of the state were deployed as rapidly as possible. It was the greatest crime in its history. From the moment the bombs had exploded, stringent security measures were taken. Even though there had been no indication that any such bombing was possible or planned, there had been preparations for emergencies, as the Red Alert response in Dublin indicated. Despite the chaos in the capital, the Gardaí and soon the army sought to seal off the way out of the city. The 5:30 train to Belfast from Connolly Station was stopped at Dundalk and searched – even though there was no useful description of the suspects. Blocks were set up on the roads to the north and in time at main junctions. The border was heavily patrolled, or as heavily patrolled as possible, which meant men on many of the unapproved roads and none on others. The Gardaí began to comb hotel and guest-house registers for likely candidates and to filter through the rising number of telephone calls reporting suspicious cars, suspicious visitors, suspicious accents. The fakes and hoaxes began almost before the last casualties reached the hospitals.

In Belfast the lists of recently stolen vehicles were forwarded to the Gardaí. The raw lists were extensive, as the Troubles had made car theft practically a cottage industry, with hundreds of vehicles taken weekly for fun or profit or paramilitary needs. The general strike tended to distract RUC attention away from Dublin, but there was evidence of full co-operation. The RUC announced security phone numbers for any information about the Dublin bombs. And, most important, they quickly traced the origin of the four cars that had been turned into bombs and despatched the results to the Gardaí. The cars, stolen in Belfast and Portadown's loyalist areas, clearly seemed to indicate a loyalist operation.

On the evening of Friday 17 May, within an hour of the first explosions, the Government met in an emergency session to be briefed by the Gardaí on existing information. Commissioner Pat Malone henceforth reported directly to the Minister for Justice, Patrick Cooney. He would report verbally or at times in writing, at first report often and then, as the pace of the investigation slowed, weekly. The meetings at the minister's office generally included the Permanent Secretary of the Department of Justice, Peter Barry, and thus allowed Cooney to keep track of the investigation. He would then report directly to a special co-ordinating Security Committee. This included Cooney and Barry and those in the Government relevant to the investigation, including the Taoiseach, Liam Cosgrave, the Minister for Defence, Patrick Donegan, and the Coalition Labour deputies Conor Cruise O'Brien and Jim Tully. The meetings were held in the Taoiseach's ante-room and were usually joined by John Kelly, secretary to the Taoiseach, who doubled as secretary to the Minister for Defence.

As the case developed, Malone usually scheduled weekly meetings with Cooney at the minister's office. These regular contacts, at times replaced by a written report, indicated the progress of the investigation. Such progress could then, if need be, come directly to the attention of the Government.

The line thus ran from the Gardaí tracing registration numbers and suspicious people up through the Garda bureaucracy to the commissioner, across to the Minister for Justice, and then to the Security Committee and if need be to the Government. Anyone on the Government side could have reversed the flow of information with queries or doubts, but this apparently never happened. The flow was one-way and was inspired and shaped by the various levels of the Garda bureaucracy: what was needed, what was wanted, what to discard or hold back, and what to send on to a higher level.

For a small country it was a formal procedure but one easily interrupted by personal initiative. In the case of the Dublin bombs, such a break in procedure apparently did not occur: the details were winnowed as they moved up without recourse to pressure for more or criticism of the results. What each level saw seemingly satisfied, and so what finally reached the Government was what was assumed was wanted or needed. And the minister, the members of the Security Committee and the Government wanted no more than they received, asked for no more. Why should they?

Obviously the minister and the Taoiseach did not need the details of routine police work or even the data flowing in from the RUC, or else they would ask. Seemingly neither they nor other members of the Government or the Dáil were sufficiently curious to request additional information.

A special Garda task force had been set up immediately in Dublin, and two hours later a second for the Monaghan incident. But over the next few days, especially crucial days if the bombers were still hidden in the Republic, all did not necessarily go as planned. The state had not really been sealed off on Friday night, could not be sealed off in any case – if the Boyne bridges and the other choke points had been blocked properly there would have been chaos – and no such plan had been intended. And for several days all the Gardaí had were the early profiles given by those who saw the cars parked: youngish men with short hair or regular features, one about twenty-four, five feet seven inches, dark, medium-cut hair, a dark jacket and dark trousers – useful but not enough for arrest or even suspicion. Moira O'Mahoney had noted that the man in the Northern car asking for directions in Westmoreland Street was about forty or forty-five, clean-shaven, five feet ten inches, with an English accent; but no one was sure that he was involved.

Really all the profiles did was to exclude more than half the Irish population. Any adult male suspects with Northern or English accents questioned over the first weekend would still have had to reek of cordite or of guilt to warrant further attention. And there was no Identikit handbill for those on the roadblocks or searching the records of guest-houses. Over the first twenty-four hours there was not really much to relay to the Minister, much less to the curious.

On 18 May, Chief Superintendent John Jay, head of the Central Detective Unit, believed the bombers to be still in the Republic. Many would continue to believe that they had gone to ground somewhere rather than driven for the border, as had the Monaghan bombers. Perhaps the Monaghan bomb had been a diversion for just such a drive, but many assumed the bombers would not take the risk – although the risks in retrospect did not seem as great as setting up a hiding-place. And such a hide would indicate even more elaborate planning, and hiding unexplained men with Northern accents in the hours after the bombs would not be an easy matter.

There were lots of suspects, lots of alarms. Some three hundred telephone alarms had to be investigated; and there would be reports of suspects from all over the country dribbling in for weeks. The Gardaí simply lacked the resources to deal with everything quickly and effectively, or at times at all. Many reports had to be ignored.

On Saturday 18 May men with Northern accents had left a car together at Connolly Station, bought tickets separately, and sat on the Belfast train in different carriages; and despite a telephone call by a concerned citizen from the station nothing was done. There were other reports called in about men with suspicious accents and cars with Northern number plates creeping off on the ferry or seen in the countryside. A car stolen from the West Street car park in Portadown was found on Dublin's north side and so became a hot candidate for the operation until it proved to be a red herring.

There was too much noise and for a time no profile to distribute. And there was the traditional chaos arising during crisis, shifting responsibilities, new assignments and the haste for results. Complicating matters too was the fact that everyone involved knew almost from the first that much of the evidence and so the ultimate results would be found on the other side of the border. At least there seemed no hesitation on the part of the RUC, already involved in tracing the cars and apparently eager to co-operate.

Conventional police routine soon began to produce results. Some of these results had been expected: the bombers were loyalist paramilitaries. Some results had not been as certain: names and profiles of those involved, UVF people from mid-Ulster. Certainly the Monaghan bomb even more than the Dublin ones had all the indications of a swift UVF terror raid organised probably out of Portadown during a time of tension in Northern Ireland.

The Monaghan car had been stolen in Portadown. The Dublin cars had been stolen in loyalist areas by loyalists – the victims were quite vague about the men who had taken their cars and held them hostage. One car had simply been taken off the street. Stealing cars at any time, much less in the middle of a general strike that stretched the security forces, was a matter of a telephone call or two and defenders sent out on the street. Who would say them nay? It was easier to stop a moving vehicle than to go to the trouble of hot-wiring a parked one; no great underground craft was needed. The RUC could barely keep up with cars taken, found, burnt out, returned, lost or used by one group of paramilitaries or another.

In Northern Ireland every paramilitary could have a car, any model, any time, and need not worry about petrol or oil; there were always other cars. Thus the trail that led to Belfast and Portadown indicated that the operation moved from north to south on a tight timetable, funnelling the operators and their devices into the Republic some time on 17 May.

However the operation had been conceived, directed, and completed, the Gardaí soon had the details of the crucial mid-point of the operation, the day of the bombs, from the first morning thefts to detonation. The RUC had generated a great deal of information out of Belfast and Portadown, although direct contact with witnesses and suspects in Northern Ireland could not so far be arranged. For their part the Gardaí soon had very firm descriptions of those directly involved in both Dublin and Monaghan; some of the data matched up with RUC information as well.

The core of the operation had been UVF "Mid-Ulster Brigade" people in Portadown, who supplied the drivers and personnel, arranged transport, safe houses, explosives, and communications, and acquired the needed technology. The descent to Dublin, and to Monaghan, began and ended in Portadown and involved loyalists long known to the RUC, the British army, the IRA, and in many cases the Gardaí.

A great deal of the violence in mid-Ulster could be traced to a small warren of streets in Portadown, the Killycomain district, stronghold of the hard men of the UVF. For them any bombs used against Catholics or nationalists would be congenial, and to them the Dublin and Monaghan bombs were not exceptional but an opportunity grasped.

By the end of the month the details concerning the events and the suspects involved from mid-morning on Friday 17 May until the moment of explosion were known to the Gardaí involved in the investigation, and leads and suspicions reached out towards further evidence and other prospects. The bombers had been not so much careless as unlucky and the police quick off the mark. From very early on the Gardaí knew most of what had happened and who had been involved, particularly the identity of eight of the individuals who had been active in the Republic.

Black Friday began with action on a request by the UVF in Portadown for help from their friends in Belfast on transport. The people in Belfast simply went out on the streets and lifted the cars in such a way that the number plates would be clean for the rest of the day, certainly the rest of the day in Dublin. No subtlety was used. Even less was apparent later in the day in Portadown when three UVF men wandered about without cover or discretion trying for a quick hijack.

Some time between eight and ten on Friday morning in Belfast a blue Ford Escort was simply driven away from Duncrue Road in the docks, to be parked later that day with a bomb in the boot in Talbot Street, Dublin. Two cars were stopped on the street in the Shankill. The first was the green Austin 1800 that would be parked in South Leinster Street. At just after nine in the morning the driver was taken out of the car in Agnes Street, blindfolded, and moved to his own home in Torrens Road, Oldpark. There he was kept under the gun. He could recall little about this when questioned later. At almost the same time in the morning the driver of the green Avenger used in Parnell Street was stopped in Torrens Road, taken out of his car, blindfolded, and moved to a nearby house. He too could remember little useful when questioned by the RUC after their almost simultaneous release at three that afternoon.

The car used in Monaghan was taken soon after half two that afternoon from the West Street car park in Portadown after an earlier attempt by three UVF people had gone awry. No great effort had been made to hide the Portadown hijacking efforts, so, unlike Belfast, the UVF people did not get away clean. The entire Monaghan part of the operation tended to be more haphazard: it was closer to home, more comfortable, less taxing, easy to make do, and so the UVF made do with less effort.

Those involved in Portadown, in the entire operation, did not seem unduly concerned about security. Who would tattle on their own, especially if vengeance were likely? So, sensibly, neither of the Belfast victims of motor theft could remember much about their captors. In Portadown only the first failed attempt was reported, but that was before the implications were fully understood. The witnesses saw only car theft, not atrocity in the making; simple crime, not a special operation. May 1974 was a time for keeping oneself to oneself. Thus there might have been other thefts, other hostages; but there were no twisted, blackened number plates to suggest this.

It is possible, even probable, that other cars stolen, hired or borrowed that day were involved, but none could be traced to the bombs. In the end the RUC had only a long list of possibles –

cars recently lost, strayed or stolen in the six counties – and none of these were ever found to be involved in the Republic. In fact once the escape car crossed the border after the Monaghan bomb, the Gardaí learned very little about the final stages of the operation. The UVF went to ground. The defenders said nothing, then or later.

For the bombers, transport was a matter of a telephone call or dropping by the West Street car park when the first attempt failed; only a few minutes and little thought need be given to mobility. It was simply another day's work at the non-hire car business, which often saw several hundred vehicles change hands over a weekend. The Dublin-bound cars had then been driven through Portadown and moved on by the UVF locals to an isolated farm not far from the border in County Armagh. The Monaghan-bound car from Portadown was moved down to another isolated farm. In both cases the explosive device, detonators and timers were waiting.

At least twenty individuals were involved, and the Gardaí very soon would have the names, not only of those who drove the cars but also those involved in the planning and preparation. Everyone in the area knew who was likely to be involved, as it was a UVF operation – and UVF operations were rarely the clockwork, precise exercises of a trained underground.

Despite the military titles and martial proclamations, the UVF was usually organised about a hard man and his local associates, who collectively had contacts with others who could supply goods or services, or themselves if need be. The size of the unit depended on what needed to be done. The British army would refer to such as the Portadown UVF as "friendly guerrilla forces". The Portadown UVF people assumed they were not merely friendly but allies, not guerrillas but defenders, the faithful shaped to preserve their way of life. They all knew each other, in many cases had known each other for years. They were organised more as a social club than a secret army, were not over-concerned about secrecy: why hide from their own friends and community, their own police and army? Even the IRA tended to know their names and record.

The British might want to apply the formulas of anti-insurgency doctrine, but the UVF, real enough, did not fit conventional texts. The Portadown UVF were the Ribbonmen and Night Riders of the present, killing and burning out the Fenians, and suddenly, unexpectedly involved in a "foreign" operation, an attack on the centre of Irish nationalism.

For the Dublin spectacular the defenders could draw on assets in place or offered. They could involve those eager to take action, drive the cars, or place the bombs, and also involve those who need only supply aid and comfort, arrange for the explosives, lend a barn, store some gear, acquire timers, or simply, like the Belfast friends, supply vehicles. The twenty Portadown names were only slightly different from those on any such list the year before or the year before that; the Troubles had brought out the hard men, and as yet attrition had not greatly adjusted the roll.

In the farmyard in south Armagh the devices were placed in the boots of the cars, but not activated. It was risky enough driving to Dublin with the several stone of explosives in each boot and the detonators to hand without having the device ticking away. The Dublin cars then drove south in convoy, and crossed the border into Monaghan on an unapproved road at Ballsmill. The drivers, as planned, used secondary roads, skirted the major towns, passed over the Boyne at Oldbridge, and motored on south past Dublin Airport, their last landmark before the rendezvous.

One at a time the cars finished up their parade from the North and pulled into the car park in front of a large and highly visible church at Whitehall. All had seemingly gone as planned, No one had stopped them, and no one was waiting for them. No one seemed to take any notice at all.

They gathered around their cars, and the first device in the blue Ford Escort was activated, the timer set running to the detonator that would set off the explosives. In this case a concentrated explosive had been procured, so that the amount used was not great. The IRA often surrounded their inner core of cutting explosives with low-grade, home-made lifting explosives often refined from a fertiliser base. In this case the UVF had good material, effective detonators, and accurate timers. The boot was closed and the second device in the green Avenger immediately activated. It took a minute or so to finish the job in the boot of the green Austin that would end in South Leinster Street.

The drivers got in and moved the cars off, carefully, for they were now hot with the clocks running. The three moved off down the Swords Road to Drumcondra, towards the centre of the city. Each was handled by the designated driver while the get-away car moved out to be in place for the escape.

It would have appeared that to drive unknown, unremarkable cars sixty-odd miles over back roads, stop once, and then drive on and park three of the cars in the middle of rush-hour Dublin traffic while the crowds were hurrying home would be a recipe for anonymity. Who would notice? Who would care? Who would remember? In any case trade craft was not a UVF asset, cover had always been a momentary matter, and most operations had been slapdash, bold, arrogant, and on the home field.

In this case the UVF had less luck: all the drivers were recognised by eye-witnesses. Eight men were noted and remembered, including those involved in Monaghan. The drivers' identities as well as their faces were soon circulated and the men soon traced and their involvement established – or established as far as the Gardaí were concerned. There had even been a Garda in the church car park, a sound witness who had seen the cars from the North and the men opening and closing the boots. Two cousins had been standing beside a bridge taking registration numbers and checking faces, looking for poachers, when two of the three bomb cars passed them moving south. The numbers were noted and the faces remembered. In Dublin and Monaghan people had noted and would remember the drivers who parked the cars in the street.

The Gardaí almost at once had eight suspects from this eye-witness testimony. And the UVF being the UVF, and Portadown security being porous, they had names and photographs to go with their witnesses' recollections. The judicial system would require the witnesses to pick a suspect out of an identity parade before real identification could be made and so hold up as hard evidence in court. That might come later, but for the moment the Gardaí knew the names of eight of those involved and, at first by implication and soon through information supplied, the names of their friends and colleagues.

The UVF team was the hard core of the Portadown movement. Many had been involved almost since the beginning in the UVF, and some would continue for some time their paramilitary activities. One of these would have a career of twenty-five years, involving numerous operations, be credited with various murders, and become notorious in police circles. In the spring of 1974 there were really no sleepers in the UVF; once the bombs were tied in to Portadown the police had a whole menu of suspects. Sources in Portadown and recourse to the Garda files kept along the border indicated in detail the names and paramilitary careers of those identified and of those involved who were not sighted in the Republic.

The UVF in mid-Ulster was a mix of hard men and their acolytes, mostly men of narrow views and a dedication to the limited ideas if not ideals of the Orange state. They found truth in their prejudices, and when threatened – as the IRA armed struggle and before that the civil rights campaign had threatened their assumptions – they were apt to strike out, vigilantes for a tradition that existed more in perception than in fact. Each accepted as basic, however, that their way of life – their innate superiority – was threatened by Catholicism and nationalism. Each felt that action must be taken.

Perhaps the most important was Billy Hanna, who was later shot dead outside his door in Lurgan on 26 July 1975 by one of his UVF colleagues, an occupational hazard in loyalist paramilitary circles, where feuds, personal rivalries, territorial arguments, suspicions and quarrels over finances regularly led to murder. Hanna hated both Catholics and the Orangemen – his grandmother was a Catholic and so the Orange Order would not have him – and found a congenial home in the UVF, more militant than any Masonic order, proper answer to his despised Catholic heritage.

Another locally famous defender and key planner was Horace

Boyle, a UVF "major" who would be killed in an attack on a dance band, the Miami Showband massacre the next year in July. Boyle made much of his titles, just as Hanna did of his new acceptance. The UVF offered a variety of returns for doing what came naturally.

Then there was Robert McConnell from south Armagh, and two brothers well known locally, Stuart and Ivor Young. All were ordinary hard men ready for what was needed. Most stayed on in Northern Ireland and in the UVF when times got difficult, but not all: the two Young brothers would move on to Scotland, where they remained safe from any enquiries. The driver of the Monaghan car, Sammy Whitten, and the UVF's explosives expert, Billy Fulton, were also known. One had been seen in Dublin, and the other had never made any secret of his activities.

All the UVF people were known in 1974, not only to the RUC but also to British military intelligence and often to the Gardaí. They were all practising paramilitaries, some were ruthless and brutal, and several had the closest links with the British military. Some had served in the Ulster Defence Regiment, and some had been on various undercover payrolls. There were few surprises to be found on the Garda list.

If the operation was a UVF affair, then there must be valid UVF reasons for risking a complex and untypical journey to Dublin. Why bomb Dublin? Why on 17 May? This tended to worry the police less than the analysts, who in any case soon had explanations for the actions of men who seldom reasoned matters out. All Irish commentators pointed out that the general strike to bring down the Sunningdale agreement, the Council of Ireland and, in passing, the new Assembly in Northern Ireland was two days old. The results remained uncertain. Did the UVF think they could make a point relevant to the strike, carry the war to the South? Did they think matters through at all?

The British government, the Northern Ireland Office and the security forces certainly had no reason to look to Dublin for anything. Sunningdale hung in the balance. Why would the British authorities bomb Dublin? There might have been reasons for some in 1972 – force Dublin to act against the IRA – but not in 1974. The loyalists would do so out of reflex, a desire to strike out at vulnerable enemies during a time of turmoil, a need to make mid-Ulster count.

It certainly seemed to many that the explosions on Friday 17 May lacked the precise timing and tuning of the earlier bombs. They were, of course, still a specific violent message, but less coercion than vengeance, less targeted on the Dublin establishment than on Irish nationalism in general. At moments of tension and crisis, especially when London refused to operate as the faithful loyalists required, the paramilitaries tended to strike at Catholics or nationalists: all were guilty.

Despite the consensus that the loyalists were to blame and the still-secret police evidence that it was the mid-Ulster UVF in particular, not all saw matters so simply. A few saw the hand of Britain – three bombs, all at once, and one in Monaghan too – but there were always those in the country who saw the hand of Britain in any catastrophe. But most then and many later focused solely on the loyalist paramilitaries. They had their reason for penetrating what Orange oratory had long proclaimed as the heart of Irish nationalism, seat of a government in collusion with the IRA, and so for bombing Dublin, a city inhabited largely by Catholics and nationalists.

The Monaghan bomb truly had the earmarks of loyalist capacity: not in sync with the Dublin bombs, the car lifted at the last minute in Portadown, a known, soft target that was close to the border and easy to reach, with a quick route back to safety. Limited skill had been required and little was displayed: the theft of transport bungled in front of witnesses, the timing off, the car hurriedly parked in front of a Protestant pub by a driver forced to move in a hurry under the eyes of witnesses. The Monaghan operation appeared hasty, more happenstance and rushed than the result of cunning and meticulous planning. The whole thrust of the operation was different, started with different transport, left from a different south Armagh farmyard, was similar only in the results and the nature of the bomb.

Those who saw a formal operation felt the Monaghan bomb might have been to divert the authorities from the Dublin group as they withdrew. If this hardly seemed convincing, then or later – the Irish authorities could only respond fully and with existing plans, no matter how many bombs were detonated throughout the countryside – there was an obvious logic to the connection. The Monaghan bomb had gone off in conjunction with the others and thus could have had operational purpose. It might simply have arisen from enthusiasm and extra material once the major thrust had been decided. It might have been an add-on that added on little but numbers on the butcher's bill. It did indicate a major and singular effort on the part of the involved: the Monaghan bomb was a UVF mid-Ulster affair, whatever the intent.

The bombs in the centre of Dublin appeared more coherently structured operationally if still difficult to rationalise politically. The three cars had detonated almost simultaneously and had been placed dead centre, one as near Leinster House as one-way traffic and parking easily permitted. The time chosen came at a moment of confusion and uncertainty in Northern Ireland and appeared coherent if less specific than the 1972 bombs. Any direct correlation with political events and loyalist reaction was often hard to find; but, given the record, the Dublin bombs fit what pattern there was. The general assumption, then, continued to be that the operation related directly to Northern events, had a coherent explanation.

The IRA might bomb all manner of targets in Northern Ireland, each, no matter how inappropriate – pub or housing estate, greengrocer's shop or hotel – falling under the heading of part of the "artificial economy" of the six counties. The Provisional IRA bombed to a lethal logic, even if too often the targets appeared rashly chosen, endangering the innocent, or worse, because ideologically suspect, endangering or destroying only Protestant targets. Leaving aside sectarian bias and the tendency of the IRA active service units to be more ruthless in London, the logic of much of the IRA campaign was easier to follow than the psychological imperatives of the sectarian acts of the loyalists. The defenders tended to act almost spontaneously and locally against a single category of available victims. This did not mean that in their own terms the Dublin bombs were not logical: they certainly seemed logical to the UVF, and so were explicable to analysis.

The 1974 bombs, however, unless they marked a beginning, something the Gardaí feared, were a singular event. Even if there had been other loyalist bombs, if the 1972 Dublin explosions were loyalist, the May event was special, consisting of a major bombing and a subsidiary bombing, and no warning at all. Surely, some felt, the event must have a singular, relevant rationale, unlike the haphazard sectarian killings of the past. And the operation was singular in that it revealed a competence not especially typical of the loyalists. The parts and phases might individually be within loyalist capacity – the theft of transport, the choice of targets, the construction of the bombs, the tracing of a withdrawal route, acquisition of detonators and timers – but the combination was no easy matter. And, most important, the concept was even more remote from loyalist practice: the idea that would impose operational shape was in a sense the most important aspect of the event and the most alien to the loyalist mind. So a few observers from the beginning looked behind the loyalists' façade. They were apt to find explanation where perhaps none was needed. Ireland of the Troubles abounds in suspected conspiracies, most imaginary but some real. In the case of the Dublin and Monaghan bombs some sought logic if not evidence beyond the loyalists.

Coherence and timing in special operations, even those controlled by professionals, are more apt to be the result of compensating errors, luck, the contingent and unforeseen. Any covert operation is inherently hampered, not enhanced, by secrecy: a cover may be necessary but there is always a substantial cost in efficiency, always, whether the SAS is involved or the UVF. Illicit operations cannot be practised as can hijack rescues or commando raids, because those involved either do not have the resources, like the IRA, or cannot create truly "illicit" conditions. Pretending to be illegal is not the same thing at all. So everyone learns on the job: no one practises with a hot car bomb.

Unconventional operations, whether state-sponsored or not, have their own dynamics. For example, regardless of the details of planning involved, the instructions given and taken, or the operational necessities, the driver with an explosive device in his car discovers that his or her priorities shift in real life. Suddenly there is an enormous urgency to find a parking place, to leave the poisoned parcel far behind, that often, if not always, overrides most other considerations.

Certainly the three Dublin drivers got into the centre of the city, but equally certainly, with time ticking away behind them in the boot, they did not seek, even if they had such a list, specific targets. Parking was difficult for everyone because of the bus strike, but for them finding a slot when driving a car bomb was not a matter of luck or convenience or proper planning but a life-or-death matter. The keen analysts who have never sat beside live explosives watching the numbers flicker down towards zero may impose more coherence on a successful operation than those involved intended.

The Dublin events indicated if not full control at least coherence: all devices timed and set simultaneously within central Dublin, all of a size and a kind. The Monaghan bomb was close enough to be in the same category. Four devastating explosions at Friday teatime, same strength, same delivery system, same operation. Someone had collected four or more stolen cars – clean until detonation – moved the operators, explosives, timers and detonators together in the cars' boots, and arranged not only for simultaneous explosions but also the simultaneous withdrawal of the Dublin drivers. It was, in the popular sense, a professional operation by those heretofore not so inclined.

The operation, technically sound, made less sense tactically. To what end was such an event organised? The loyalists did not need elaborate rationales, but if the operators were competent in one matter would they not have been in others? The reasoning behind the event must be coherent as well. Why Friday 17 May 1974? The analysts without access to the bombers devised rationales that tended to give the event necessary coherence: no one likes murder by compensating accidents, assassination by the demented. There should be a reason why thirty-three people died, so many lives ruined. There should be an overriding purpose that made sense.

The obvious step was to link the explosions with events of the moment. Yet even if professionals or at least skilled loyalists were involved, the bombs were unlikely to have been deployed with negligible preparations and so to coincide with the general strike. In fact the general strike only gradually assumed epic proportions. During the early days of the strike no one knew if it would be more than gesture, least of all those involved. Few of those involved could really be sure that in withholding their services a crisis would evolve from the inability or unwillingness of the Northern Ireland Office and the British army to break the effort with force. The Northern Secretary, the Prime Minister and certainly the British military commanders all denied then and later that force would work, but up to the strike no one had felt that any response would be necessary. Many, all the visible authorities, all of the media, all of the sensible, expected little from the strike. Those involved did have real hopes, but loyalist paramilitaries or any unspecified British professionals could not have foreseen a need for bombs during the first few days of the strike.

Thus the bombs came not because of the general strike but contemporaneously. And so there was far less cause and effect than in December 1972, when, however simple-minded, the purpose was to coerce a Government engaged in considering anti-IRA measures. The Dublin policy as perceived by the loyalists and their friends in 1972 was long-standing, and the debate on the Offences Against the State Act was highly visible and presented the bomb planners with fair warning of target dates. The 1972 bombs were meant to punish Dublin for collusion no matter what, and to help herd the reluctant Irish establishment towards repressing the IRA – and this seemingly occurred.

The bombs of November and December 1972 were not simply symbolic. Damage must have been expected, since minimal care was taken to ensure that there were no casualties: two men running out of a lane shouting as they fled and a warning telephoned in Belfast almost as the bombs were scheduled to detonate. These might be an indication that loyalists or that less skilled personnel were involved, or that those who shaped the events were less than competent or merely callous. Still, the 1972 bombing had an obvious overriding purpose.

The lack of rationale in 1974, the vacuum in political planning, tended therefore to suggest the loyalists operating alone – more efficiently than in the past, but this was not beyond reason, The Gardaí knew the UVF had been operational; but this did not mean they had not acted in conjunction with others more professional. There might be a puppet-master pulling the UVF operational strings; but again the Gardaí had no evidence, nor did those who suspected the British have good reasons. If these other "professionals" were British special operators, authorised or rogue, their operational rationales were grounded in innocent arrogance, personal bias, and the lure of the deed. The loyalists might be operational amateurs, but any such "professionals" would have to be ludicrously innocent of Irish political reality.

What this meant was that in theory the more professional and therefore sophisticated the bombs were operationally, the less likely they could have been planted by any of the suspects, UVF or British. In theory the UVF lacked the technical skills and the British the inane audacity to bomb without tactical or strategic purpose. And yet there were thirty-three dead, and to no visible tactical purpose. So, if there was a conspiracy beyond the mid-Ulster UVF, there must have existed a mix of capacities and confusion. This is a common conjunction underground, where perception encourages the ruthless and desperate to unconventional means rather than accept injustice. And in nearly all unconventional conflicts, sooner or later, the legitimate find the lure of the illicit and covert overwhelming, often discarding even rationality in pursuit of operational advantage. The British could have been involved, no matter how irrational the connection.

All unconventional conflicts evolve from an asymmetrical violent dialogue with all the numbers and tangibles on one side – that of the state – and the other, the rebels, capable of persisting because their perceptions and aspirations cannot easily be destroyed by force alone. For the rebel, secrecy is crucial and costly. The rebel must hide those aspirations with a cover, strike with unorthodox means against the arrayed tangibles.

In all secret wars, all internal wars, all wars of national liberation waged by covert means, many civil wars and some campaigns on the margins of real wars, the distinction between orthodox and irregular, the permitted and the illicit, the involved and the innocent, is eroded. The weak must strike where they can. And the strong find concentration difficult against the perceptions and ideas of the weak. Each state is apt to respond differently: some kill all who might be weak, and others display enormous firepower to intimidate the hidden.

Few states, no matter how legitimate their governance nor civil their culture, long deny themselves the perceived benefits of covert operations for seeking out those with subversive ideas, those loyal to a secret army operating underground. To do so secrecy is required, to protect their own, but this is almost certain to permit the illicit. Secrecy does not simply *encourage* the evolution of the conflict into a dirty war but ensures this result. And dirty wars are so because those involved, through incompetence and arrogance, accept as practical the illusion that necessity allows the violation of norms. Necessity, however, need be covered so that the war can be denied, the benefits of legitimacy and righteousness maintained.

So those who can be plausibly denied are allowed, encouraged or ordered to descend into a world where, since everything is hidden, anything is permitted. And what is permitted, the violation of the law, the murder of classes and categories, torture and terror, can still be plausibly denied by those in public view. Soon, if not from the first, responsibility up and responsibility down is blurred and lost at the cover line – the point where one no longer needs to know, where no one wants to know and so should know that ignorance is not innocence but complicity.

No British politicians, few British soldiers, would have authorised the detonation of car bombs in the middle of Dublin, sent men to kill the innocent. The English, more than most, have long benefited, deservedly, from a national stereotype that stresses fair play, restraint, moderation, the love of the law and the institutionalisation of justice. The English play by the rules, even if rules they devised, rules arising as a result of a heritage of democracy and justice hard-won. Such an assessment is not merely to be found in school primers or patriotic speeches but the assumptions of many, and often those who seek to wrest the same rights from the British by recourse to a gun.

It is thus no easy matter to see those at the core of the British system responsible for the murder of innocents on the streets of a friendly country – nor would many of the everyday people be so involved: the constable, the soldier, the clerk in the government office. If, however, there were those engaged in dirty tricks, it would not be the first time that law had ceded to those who offered order or the first time that the irregular found opportunity within the British system. Those who write the rules often feel impelled to adjust them to ensure appropriate results, which are, after all, the purpose of rules.

In 1972 there had been evidence that the bombing operation had been shaped by some in the security forces. Those directly involved may or may not have been at one remove, but a great many people in Ireland and elsewhere felt that the act was not beyond the control that the security forces in Northern Ireland had. In 1974 as the Garda investigation continued, not only did evidence accumulate that the UVF had been responsible but circumstances also suggested that the idea, perhaps not only the details but also aspects of the operation, could again be traced to the British security forces.

If so, this time the logic for such bombs was not compelling, the analysis of any advantageous results difficult to follow, and consequently an assumption that the concept of such a guided UVF operation was most probably devised by those far down the chain. These locals could only have acted out of innocent arrogance. Still, even those in positions of considerable responsibility in the British establishment had long shown an innocent arrogance about Irish affairs. Much of the British establishment exhibited a flat learning curve, never realising the enormous community of interests between London and Dublin. Many, a great many, and not simply on the back benches or smaller city offices, found long-held bias about the Paddies, their feckless behaviour, their collusion with mad-dog gunmen, comforting and so more than ample foundation for policy. And surely some of these were active in Northern Ireland, in touch with the UVF? And, of course, all of these would lack any empathy with the Irish – not a British failing alone but a flaw that made a war where perceptions play as large a role as tangibles far more difficult to pursue. They, the operators, might easily see the UVF as guerrillas and the IRA as an extension of the Irish Republic.

So a few in the right place with the wrong views could well have shaped the UVF to what seemed a good purpose and one subsequently too delicate to discuss or to acknowledge. Certainly the loyalists of the UVF had been involved, men intimately known to the British authorities, often on the British payroll, though as creatures, converted terrorists or "friendlies". At times too the British had created loyalist organisations for special purposes, as with John McKeague's "Red Hand Commandos", and at other times had been content to nudge the paramilitaries into useful directions.

Usually for the UVF a wink was ample, and often unneeded: who required rationale to strike at Ulster's enemies? And for the UVF, as the Gardaí knew, the deed had been done and done with despatch. For the defenders and even for the police the focus in May and June 1974 was on the operators, not a conspiracy, not on analysis based on logic and speculation but on evidence.

Chapter VI

For the analysts the crucial question was the shape of loyalist involvement; for the Gardaí this was less important than the guilt of the loyalists. The trail that led almost immediately to Portadown opened into a pool of fundamentalist, loyalist activists. The eight names became twenty.

The UVF, unlike the large militia organisations of defenders that had arisen easily in Belfast, especially as the IRA campaign accelerated, was not a mass organisation, not interested in politics. These mass groups often had at the core a collection of those ready, often eager, to take active measures, often under various cover names. The UVF, a core without a surrounding mass, still legal, used the names Protestant Action Force and Protestant Action Group to take responsibility for their "military" operations.

All the loyalist militia groups had a paramilitary flavour – uniforms, formations, titles – and the UVF was no different. There was a heritage of costume, ritual and office from the Orange lodges, and there was the obvious example of the hated IRA.

The small UVF groups, linked by association and acquaintance rather than recruited under a grand banner, were often less than discreet in their operations. Few involved had felt great need to be discreet in their Stormont state. They had evolved in 1971–72 around certain individuals who could not or did not seek mass support but only a chance to act. These local vigilantes were covered – often literally – with historical symbols and emboldened by what was perceived as contemporary need unserved by the conventional unionist politicians.

The first on the scene, even before the Troubles, the UVF emerged in various transmutations as the most militant and the most lethal of all the loyalist groups. And all the while the UVF remained legal, allied, so the members assumed, to Stormont and the Crown and, with their state gone, allied to the system, the security forces, the traditions of a Protestant people beleaguered in their corner of a small island.

As "defenders" there was minimal UVF concern with mass mobilisation, political action, protest politics, or moderation. And the best defence was to intimidate the perceived enemy, the neighbouring, Catholic nationalist enemy, to use whatever means physical force offered. The UVF was action-oriented. The members were not averse to involvement in raising funds, exercising power in their own areas, dabbling in extortion and fringe commercial transactions; but the formal purpose of the UVF was to deploy violence against Irish nationalism, loosely defined. Between actions the organisation drifted, a few classes, some meetings, but mostly waiting for stimulus, provocation, a likely target.

One did not become a member of the UVF simply to march in Orange parades or to applaud politicians. Many of the hard men of the UVF in Belfast could be pointed out standing in pub doors, drinking in the corner, or with their hard-eyed colleagues driving in unconventionally acquired cars slowly down the lane. Rough, ruthless, without education, they had found a vocation that offered personal power, the excitement of the illicit, recourse to the gun, and ready money, and all this under a patriotic banner.

A few found charm in authorised killing beyond the excitement of operations and matured into psychopaths, but most were men who felt authorised to kill, who considered pogroms proper and murder of Fenians no sin but a Protestant duty. In different wars, real wars, they often made good soldiers, and in Ulster made good neighbours, seemingly decent men but for their commitment to force as a means of stressing superiority over the others, the Catholics, which by 1974 was hardly visible in any other way.

Some, particularly in Belfast, made a good thing out of the UVF or the UDA, lived a full, fat life until a harder man came along or at times the IRA showed up with a map drawn by a rival. The difference in Portadown was the size of the town and the scope of control. Belfast offered poorly policed districts but Portadown only one; Belfast offered lucrative pickings, Portadown fewer opportunities; some locals even moved in on Belfast opportunities rather than wait isolated in their own district.

The UVF hard men grew alike as time passed: fewer idealists, fewer concerned only with defending their own. And as time passed, new defenders would arrive to remove the corrupt, revitalise the UVF, kill the others. In 1974 the first levee was still in place.

The hard men around which the UVF was usually organised made alliances and agreements and at times accepted the theory of centralised control. The leaders might then appear at a press conference with military titles, dark glasses and self-created uniforms to talk of "operations" and "units" and even, as a few grew more sophisticated, political programmes. Yet the UVF was not a secret army, not a conventional organisation at all; involved in crime but not really a criminal organisation, it was a defender of the state but dedicated to violating the law.

The defenders felt they were aligned with the authorities, their own, the British, to take acts that might embarrass the more refined, more visible agencies of the Crown. In the process there was no point in denying the fiscal benefits that might accrue from such activities or even the influence that the gun in society might bring, but the real purpose was to intimidate the disloyal. And beyond this avowed purpose lay the need for the reassurance that such violence brought.

Power came to those with guns, but not legitimacy, nor the capacity to organise Ulster. Even those who sought to exercise excessive power in local fiefs ran great risks. Jim Hanna, once UVF commander, who had claimed privately the responsibility for the 1972 bombs, was shot and killed in Mansfield Street, off the Shankill Road, Belfast, on 31 March 1974, by his own. He was one of the many lost to internal suspicions and jealousy, quarrels over spoils and fear of penetration. Without the discipline of a compelling ideology or a conventional form, without authority at the top, the UVF, no matter how small, was more of an alignment of the like-minded than an organisation.

The UVF was the legal cover, a symbol rather than a guild with dues and duties and minutes. It was a point of action, pulsing with the variations in events and provocation, that drew the desperate from the vicinity. The magnet was usually a few eager to act whose intensity attracted others. Action both deterred the cautious and attracted the bold. The interim between events allowed a certain coherence to evolve; but the UVF existed in 1974 more as a curious working-class social club with a limited membership dedicated to killing and to the benefits so derived. It was not a covert revolutionary or even vigilante cell, not part of an underground army, and so not – until the bombs went off – a likely candidate for such a paramilitary operation.

In mid-Ulster the members knew each other, trusted the sound and dependable, met at the local, spoke of threats and possibilities, heard rumour and vulnerabilities reported, and from time to time organised an action. Sometimes with drink taken the deed could be the enthusiasm of the moment. At other times planning and care came on top of long discussions on a perceived provocation. Over time those involved drifted in and out of commitment, found other interests or stayed in an unexpected vocation that increasingly dominated their life. Some, like Billy Hanna, found a home, others a stopping-place for violence before they moved on to safer pursuits in Scotland or England or even mid-Armagh.

The UVF appeared, self-generated, where the like-minded needed title and authentication, and persisted with the continued provocation and the commitment of the few. Certain localities, like Portadown, had become core areas. By 1974 the town was at the apex of a triangle of violence, Dungannon–Portadown–Armagh, where various loyalist paramilitaries operated against vulnerable targets. The UVF had evolved into an essential part of a general loyalist effort and, if not welcome by many, was tolerated by their own as defenders. And aid and comfort could be sought not only from other UVF units but from other loyalists in parts of Ulster known to the members. Ulster was small, the loyalist universe substantial. Those ready to support operations were easy enough to find. So the UVF evolved into a scattered fraternity of activists constantly in touch with other defenders and the sympathetic, but seldom on active duty. Organised more like a social club with actions instead of matches, the members met in slack periods of the schedule in pubs or on the street. They had little need of long-term planning. Their membership expanded or declined in relation to prospects and provocation.

Their operations were haphazard if effective, requiring little more than would be needed to take the club to an away football game in rival territory. Mostly the UVF responded to the climate of the times, the needs of the moment, the discovery of opportunity – almost always a chance to strike at Catholic victims during a moment of general or particular frustration. Some UVF operations, especially in Belfast, were often focused on acquiring the funds and material to allow such action, and in time mid-Ulster UVF was little different. The defenders became concerned with creating zones of control and profit. One well-known UVF hard man, Eddie Sayers, "brigadier" for mid-Ulster, even managed to appear in living colour on television in August 1987 on "The Cook Report". Ignorant of the secret camera, he made an extortion demand that indicated the nature of some UVF "actions". By then the early days were long gone and the opportunities for profit not to be so easily ignored.

But such extortion demands, the rackets, the illegal collections and tolerated theft, the organised crime aspect of the UVF's black economy, was erected on the back of real sectarian attacks. These were usually the result of the few, inspired as always by provocation or opportunity. In effect, when two or three members of the UVF were gathered together, the moment might prove adequate for a call to action and thus lead to the swift structuring of an operation: transport arranged, arms gathered, volunteers notified, a plan accepted, a drive-by shooting to be done that night. The UVF was often a vigilante posse in waiting, defenders of the past, protectors of rights long lost and a history misread. They made no effort to hide their views, which in any case were hardly unique, or to hide their associations or associates. The members in the murder triangle in 1974 were not over-concerned about secrecy. Why hide from their own friends and community, their own police and army? And so they did not hide; what member of a secret army would have *UVF Portadown* tattooed on his arm? In any case the UVF was legal until October 1975, and so there was no real need to hide membership, only the extent of operations and the details of the black economy. Everyone knew who they were.

The UVF expected only toleration from their allies, the police and British army, and when this was not given felt once more betrayed. The British might want to apply the doctrine of anti-insurgency to the UVF, but the group did not fit conventional texts. They simply drew on existing assets. For the Dublin spectacular of 1974 they could draw on those assets, involve those eager to take action. All were sound people, long known; some might not even be in the UVF, only co-operative.

In the early seventies there were all sorts of UVF defenders in the Portadown area, between one and two hundred associated in some way at any time. British military intelligence once estimated that there were in the area 127 known UVF people and that about 20 per cent of these were active. All bureaucracies like numbers, even of part-time friendly guerrillas – especially of friendly guerrillas. The UVF did not care if the British counted their numbers or kept an eye on their activities. They saw no conflict in their role in the UVF with membership of the Ulster Defence Regiment or as intelligence assets for the British army: all were traditional and vital roles.

The UVF volunteers were not, however, always available for hazardous duty. For some the UVF was more an Orange Order or a social club, offering the odd night out in pub plotting against the Fenians. Membership was not a late vocation, as with Hanna, but a social arrangement. Others found that practicalities limited their commitment to action. Not everyone wanted to sit in the front seat of a stolen car with a borrowed revolver waiting for someone – anyone – to come out of a Catholic housing estate on the way to the pub. And not everyone wanted to drive a car bomb to Dublin. The result was that at any time those at the centre were seldom more than a dozen or so. The men in Portadown (for there were no women defenders) shared mostly a commitment to action undiluted by legal restraints or often by common sense. They had closed minds, but not disturbed ones. These were the volunteers for violence, those who could be counted on to drive bombs to Dublin, shoot Catholics, initiate action. They were intimate with the local, the provincial, had short views, simple views, and were dedicated to lethal solutions made legitimate by rationalisations buttressed by the symbols of the UVF, the toleration of their own, and the misreading of their tradition.

Billy Hanna was in a way the most enthusiastic mid-Ulster recruit, who found at last in the UVF a role and a place that allowed him to meld his hatred of his Catholic grandmother and of the Orange Order. Born on 27 September 1948 into a labourer's family, he found life difficult. After school he got a job in a shoe-box factory in Banbridge and moved to the Mourneview estate in Lurgan. He had been in the Ulster Defence Regiment, but that had not been enough. The UVF in Portadown took him, and he found congenial company and a comforting role.

In the UVF he revealed a natural talent for armed conspiracy, and discovered a vocation. Times of turmoil allow the untutored an opportunity that static society may deny. Revolutionary armies have free entry and promotion based only on acquired skills: no accreditation needed, no education, no influential friends. Those who can do the work are given the work. So too with the UVF, where the work was simple but the rewards for the limited considerable. And so Billy Hanna gave lectures on Monday nights on bomb-making to his fellow-defenders, and helped plan the Dublin operation.

Not only was Hanna now a member of the UVF but he also associated with the British army's intelligence operations – he assumed as a colleague, even as his handlers treated him as an asset run for their own purpose. From an anonymous employee of a shoe-box factory he became a figure of substance, recognised as a UVF hard man, trusted colleague of British intelligence, an unquestioned success.

The UVF, if it did not answer all questions for Billy Hanna, did in time supply a final answer. Some of his colleagues felt that he was an agent of some sort. In the loyalist underground, suspicion was easily raised, quickly fed, and became an imperative to act. So Billy Hanna was shot dead outside his door in Lurgan in 1975 by two of his UVF colleagues. Hanna had been in his limited way typical of the UVF and its amorphous role in the Troubles. Those who played their own parts, like Hanna, often did so at a cost.

One of those who stood and waited for Hanna that day in Lurgan was his colleague in the Dublin operation Horace Boyle – "Major" Boyle of the UVF. Boyle was well known, used his title, flaunted his membership of the UVF, and was present at the funerals of his colleagues, even of a few of those who many suspected had died at his hands. There in the graveyard standing as a paramilitary major amid his own army, he ostentatiously positioned himself near the RUC, his police.

Boyle, like Hanna, came to a spectacular end, equally unplanned. On 31 July 1975 a UVF unit had stopped the minibus of the Miami Showband outside Banbridge, County Down. Inside were six members of the group, who had been playing in Northern Ireland for thirteen years with considerable success but were, as far as the UVF were concerned, cover for the smuggling of IRA arms. The UVF intended to kill the group by pretending to search the vehicle as a UDR patrol and then planting a bomb under the driver's seat. This would blow up the van later inside the Republic. The operation collapsed when the device exploded prematurely as Horace Boyle and Wesley Somerville were slipping it into place. The van was devastated by the explosion, which killed the two UVF men and frightened the others into a wild burst of shots and then flight. In the hasty shooting the UVF survivors managed to kill only three of the six musicians, who lay stunned and scattered on the ground. The mutilated bodies of Boyle and Somerville were left on the scene. Both were easily identified, not only because the RUC found an arm bearing the tattoo *UVF Portadown* but also because the UVF hastily issued a bulletin to give their version of the event.

Wesley Somerville was already on RUC records because of his acquittal in 1974 of an attempt to hold bakery workers hostage and then drive their van loaded with explosives into a Catholic housing estate in Coalisland, County Tyrone. Boyle was even better known. Both were part-time members of the Ulster Defence Regiment. In this case the clues and a tip-off led beyond Boyle and Somerville to the arrest and conviction of the leader of the UVF group, 19-year-old Raymond Crozier, an optical worker, and 25-year-old Roderick McDowell, both from Lurgan.

It is of course one thing for the police to know of the inclination of loyalists like McDowell and Crozier and another to prove their involvement in crime. Many nationalists felt that too often the lines between the Ulster Defence Regiment, the RUC and the paramilitaries were blurred. Certainly the British and the RUC, especially those in direct contact with the mid-Ulster paramilitaries, kept tabs on a shifting group of known militants. Again the nationalists felt that the security forces were doing more than just monitoring them.

Everyone already knew the activists. There was David Mulholland of Portadown, who, having driven one of the Dublin cars, moved on to England in 1975. There was Stuart Young and, more important, his brother Ivor Young. The latter was suspected of involvement in the bombing of McGurk's Bar in Belfast on 14 December 1971. The explosion killed fifteen Catholics; but the authorities at the time had insisted, despite the evidence, that it was an IRA mistake. The evidence was refined towards this end, but both the British army and the RUC knew that it had been a loyalist bomb. The Young brothers remained suspects for various UVF operations, but nothing was proved. In time both left Northern Ireland for Scotland – a refugee and sometimes arena for UVF members.

Another of the Portadown people who went to Scotland was Billy Fulton. He had been the quartermaster, carefully collecting fertiliser and making bombs under the watchful eye of the security forces. In Scotland, still active for the UVF, he was arrested and convicted of an explosives offence.

Samuel Whitton, who drove the Monaghan car bomb, did not have to cross the water to find trouble, and was arrested and sentenced to life imprisonment for sectarian murder as well as to fourteen years on an arms charge.

One of the more famous loyalists, Robin Jackson, regularly at UVF funerals and commemorations, was always a suspect but never a defendant. In fact at one point in April 1977 he was not charged, the court was told, because of "operational reasons". Such reasons indicated that he had taken more care with his arrangements than Whitton. In fact Jackson remained untouched but always visible on the margin of the dirty war, suspect but invulnerable. He might be a "friendly guerrilla" to the British but many suspected him as the Crown's criminal.

The complexities of the loyalist underground were obvious: part criminal and part paramilitary, at times in the service of the security forces as spies, informers or provocateurs and at times operating independently, always with an eye on the main chance and always eager to defend through sectarian murder. All of this in 1974 was less clear than it would be in later years, and already the muddle of the dirty war was becoming a fact of life for the RUC and for the Gardaí.

As the years passed, evidence at various trials, media stories, rumour and leaks combined to persuade many that, as the IRA had claimed, the loyalist paramilitaries were British surrogates, co-opted for dirty tricks. This belief, not unwarranted in some documented cases, was unshaken by the growing number of UVF people who ended in prison because of – not despite – the actions of their Ulster police. Yet some did not end in jail, or not at once, or not for long. A senior Belfast UVF figure in touch with Portadown, William "Frenchie" Marchand, who was suspected of stealing the Belfast cars used for the 1974 bombs, remained free until caught up in the "supergrass" trials, where he forgave his accuser but the UVF announced that the man would be killed if he could be found in his English haven. And the informers' evidence for both republicans and loyalists proved revealing but legally faulty. In 1987 Marchand's luck ran out. Standing outside the UVF offices in Shankill Road in Belfast, he was shot and killed by the Provisional IRA.

Other defenders, like Robert McConnell, a member of both the UVF and the UDR from south Armagh, suffered a similar fate. McConnell, one of the prime planners of the Dublin 1974 operation, was shot by the IRA in April 1976. Generally the IRA tried to keep a watch on loyalist paramilitaries. The segregation of the communities often made this difficult but hardly prevented the accumulation of data on membership. The IRA tried to avoid the appearance if not the reality of shooting loyalists, always Protestants, because their operations were anti-Catholic. It was more congenial to pick loyalists who could be classified as British agents rather than misguided Protestants, for non-sectarian criteria had to be maintained in Provo targeting, in theory if not in fact. The IRA had to defend its own even if they were almost all Catholics. It was difficult to wage a non-sectarian war in a partitioned, sectarian society.

In 1974 all these defenders of the UVF and many more were on someone's list, often a list of informers, often a payroll of one security force or another, and were known to the RUC, to the British military intelligence and often to the Gardaí as practising paramilitaries. Several were ruthless and especially brutal. Several did not survive, but one by 1993 had run up an enormous if unverifiable list of victims. None had hesitated at setting car bombs amid Dublin crowds.

A few of the constant killers would develop into psychopaths, but in 1974 most of the UVF defenders simply gave themselves military cover for sectarian violence. Killing Fenians – random male Catholics – seemed almost respectable, especially so if done by the historic UVF. And if the IRA could kill with car bombs, why not the UVF? Certainly many of the mid-Ulster UVF, whatever else, felt their cause just and their gunman careers proper.

Some were involved with the security forces even when at cross-purposes. In May 1974 the degree of such involvement was not always clear to the public, and often not to those involved, the British officers or the UVF defenders. It was certainly not clear to the authorities in the Republic or to the nationalists in Ulster. Some suspect that every member of the UVF was a surrogate for the British, as did the Provisional IRA, while others were inclined to credit the RUC and to a lesser degree the British army with discretion in the inevitable tangle created by penetrating an underground. Thus in 1972 the immediate response to the December bomb – hardly anyone remembered the November bomb, even the next month, or the January 1973 bomb – had been the suspicion that the British had been directly involved. This seemed more logical than using loyalist surrogates, even if it violated avowed British principles and policies. Many in Ireland had long exposure to Britain adjusting the rules, so that even bombs in Dublin seemed within reason.

There were those who felt that the involvement might have been at one remove, but still 1972 was seen as skilfully, professionally done, because of the timing if nothing more. The 1974 Dublin explosions seemingly required, even more than the 1972 attacks, sophisticated, meticulous military operators, i.e. professionals not found in the UVF. And yet the rationale for any such explosion seemed less sophisticated, less professional – more loyalist. And the trail led not towards the security forces, who had the skills but surely would not bomb without reason, but almost at once to the mid-Ulster UVF – those who lacked the skills but had the motive.

As the days passed from the spring into the summer of 1974, the trail, so promising, began to grow cold. Except for the investigating officers, there was no urgency. After the Dublin funeral of many of the victims, the story began to slide away into small articles on the claims for damage and the fear of loss of custom by Dublin merchants, and other matters filled the newspapers and evening television programmes. For all but the survivors and their families there were other pressing matters to consider. The media showed an absence of progress reports.

And there was no further progress. There would soon be a need for many of the Gardaí involved to return to normal duties.

In part because the case had so swiftly dropped out of the newspapers, as had happened in 1972, in part because of the secrecy of a continuing investigation, and in part because those who do not ask are not told, much detail was never published. Much detail never reached the Government, the Security Committee, or the minister. And the media did not press the Gardaí.

The residue of the explosions was examined to determine the nature of the device, and evidence was sent to Northern Ireland as well, where the British military had an opportunity to check the material. The Irish public was not told of the nature, size, components or origin of the bombs, beyond the few immediate guesses offered by the Gardaí on 17 May. One officer said approximately twenty pounds each and another guessed three pounds all told of high-quality explosives. Nothing more was forthcoming. No one seemed interested in more details. No one asked in public. If more were done by forensic scientists, by the search teams, by those in contact with the RUC, no one in the Gardaí felt obliged to reveal such progress to the media, and no one in the Government felt the need to enquire about such activities. And no one in RTE or the newspapers, not even one bold journalist, seemed inspired to investigate beyond the official and increasingly rare report of progress. This was the case even as sound police work, luck and the RUC combined to give the details of the day. These details melded to make a case that convinced those in the Gardaí who were involved in pursuing the suspects. It was, however, not yet a case that would stand up in court.

Within a few weeks the Gardaí had a clear idea of what had taken place on Friday 17 May 1974 – at least from the time the first vehicle was stolen in Belfast until the moment the bombs detonated – and who had been involved. All those directly involved had been from the UVF Mid-Ulster Brigade, centred at Portadown, those who for several years had supplied the active service people for operations. Without question, the Gardaí discovered that these defenders had been responsible for the May atrocity. So they knew and the RUC knew, but not the

Government nor the public. The UVF knew but remained quiet, as did all the security forces in the North, all the "supergrass" informers and all those eager with revelations.

The 1974 bombings, if not a closed case, were for years quietly forgotten, a line in the chronology of the Troubles, the greatest crime in the history of the state now a passing mention in histories, remembered only by the survivors.

Chapter VII

Much had to be organised by the UVF, considered, collected and assigned for at least twenty people to be directly involved on Friday 17 May and another group on the edges to have been aware that a serious operation was considered. For the UVF it was a unique operation. Any cross-border attack was considered high-risk penetration into alien and hostile territory; even nearby Monaghan was uncongenial.

An attack that required three simultaneous car bomb explosions in the capital city a hundred miles into enemy territory was a special and highly unusual challenge. The 1972–73 bombs had certainly supplied the most crucial need: the idea. And the success of the December 1972 explosions had indicated the returns that such an operation might offer – seldom a very high consideration for the UVF, content to strike at local and convenient symbols. And the operational details were daunting for those previously content with such provincial forays. In the spring of 1974 a strike against the Council of Ireland authorised by the Sunningdale agreement was congenial, especially with the prospect of strike action by the loyalist workers. The usual murder of a local Catholic was hardly as appropriate a venture as an attack on the enemy capital, one that had been successful before and one that lay within the assumed capacities of the UVF.

And there were always those to give aid and comfort. Some of those outside the inner circle of the UVF had real experience in such matters. One man with a handful of timers and the idea of a Dublin raid might be all the spark the UVF needed even for what appeared a highly complex operation.

For Dublin there were three bomb cars to be driven, loaded, to the target area. There would have to be sufficient transport to collect the drivers, and a way out. Everyone had to be at the right place at the right time, to leave Portadown together, to collect the bombs near the border, to reach the assembly point north of Dublin, and for three drivers to find parking spots in the centre of the city with the timer running in the boot. Then, with little margin for confusion, the rendezvous for the escape had to be made, whatever the ultimate arrangements. Only the bomb cars could be hot; and all involved had to have a cover story, just in case.

While the operation need not go like clockwork – except for the last minutes, when the bombs were fused and the timer running – considerable planning was required. This might mean that the UVF had such resources to hand, unsuspected, unused, and not to be deployed again. It might also mean that the crucial original idea for the foray and some of the required steps and action agenda might have been offered by more professional individuals – real or rogue operators. It might even mean that along with such comfort might have come the offer of aid: aid in acquiring the components of the devices or aid in going to ground after the detonation. What was not required was volunteers for action: the UVF had those to hand and would call on some twenty defenders, most of the active men in the Mid-Ulster Brigade.

Once the three bombs went off, the UVF trail disappeared. The Gardaí did not know how the UVF people were withdrawn, or whether there had been a safe haven used until the hunt eased off, or anything about other cars and other people south of the border. The UVF people eventually all showed up back in mid-Ulster, quietly confident that the most lethal and complex operation by loyalist paramilitaries was an unqualified and secret success. How could they assume otherwise? And what could the Gardaí do even with their list of names? Ask for RUC help? What would the RUC do: seek out UVF people who might be involved in a security operation, question UVF people who had committed no crime in Northern Ireland?

At first the Gardaí assumed this would be the case. Ireland was in turmoil. The Government was appalled, and no less so by the willingness of the Northern Ireland Office to talk to such loyalists in the middle of the general strike. This dismay, of course, delighted the UVF, just as had the clean sweep into Dublin and Monaghan in their bomb cars. All told, it had been a most successful month, and the UVF in mid-Ulster savoured in secret their covert operation; no need to take credit. The UVF defenders felt secure beyond touch of the Irish or their own, a secret army secretly at work. Except of course that both the Gardaí and the RUC knew many of the secrets.

After the first returns of RUC co-operation, the Gardaí noticed a lack of new information, no more secrets revealed. They discovered that none of the UVF suspects so far identified had been questioned. In fact the RUC was no longer forthcoming, and the British army had never been. Apparently the RUC suspected that the British military and intelligence might have reasons not to be forthcoming and so did not push their investigation. Those in the British army showed a lack of curiosity; no one anywhere in the security forces wanted to find evidence that there was official backing for a massacre in the streets of a friendly country. Better not to ask, not to pursue the Garda request; better let matters rest if this were possible. Those in the RUC involved ended their investigation – after all, Dublin had made no formal requests to the Northern Ireland Office, so no co-operation was required. If the Gardaí wanted more aid and comfort, then they could go through channels.

In three months the Gardaí got no further than they had in the first ten days. No channels to Northern Ireland were opened. The Government learned nothing of the list of suspects. All the alleged perpetrators were in Northern Ireland, where they might or might not have official protection but where they remained untouched by the RUC and beyond reach of the Gardaí. The Gardaí on the ground, turning over photographs, collecting data, talking to witnesses, writing up reports, found that there was no more to be done in the field. They could not get to the UVF, much less contemplate any hidden hands. No one in authority in Dublin seemed curious. There was no urgency about their lack of progress. The minister did not demand results, nor the

Security Committee, nor even members of the Dáil. Those engaged in the investigation realised that no step had been taken by the authorities to secure RUC co-operation.

In fact nothing was happening. The investigation had nothing more to investigate, and so officers were moved, duties shifted, and gradually the effort shut down. The case was never closed – murder cases are never formally closed – but within a few months the files were filed, the records were tidied, and the last officers shifted to more pressing duties. For nearly twenty years matters would rest there, an unproven case against the UVF cut short, if not unexpectedly, by lack of Northern co-operation – co-operation unsought, quite unexpectedly, by the appropriate authorities. The case had disappeared into the gap in the bureaucracy between the Gardaí and the Government.

Some of the Gardaí involved were bitter that the perpetrators were going to escape, and that those charged to find them were going to be blamed. They never forgave or forgot. They would see that when the time came the record was clear, if unofficial. As for the rest, those in power and those who would be, those in the Dublin establishment and those in Belfast and London, had other priorities.

The Dublin bomb cases had never really been forgotten, but what could be done? The prospect of actually indicting the specific culprits, culprits still unknown outside Garda circles, grew very remote. There were also a few who felt that evidence was accumulating of the possibility that the British security forces had been involved, certainly in 1972, perhaps in 1974. In the latter case only the Gardaí knew for certain that the UVF had been primarily responsible, but increasingly there were those who felt that the British army and intelligence had shaped the suspected loyalists to their own use.

The bombs of 1972 and 1974 became counters in the campaign against British dirty tricks, and so were often remembered by nationalists not as a UVF atrocity but as an exercise in state-sponsored terror. Always cited, never explained, the bombs became part of the litany of grievance. No one seemed able to prove anything, even as more analysts considered

British involvement as possible; the speculative possibility was founded not on evidence but on other revelations about British actions in response to the IRA's armed struggle.

Twenty years of a brutal, dirty war had presented observers with an array of examples of the fact that in such matters no one involved, including the RUC and the British army, had denied themselves the perceived advantages of covert, illicit operations. The authorities in Belfast and London compounded their problem when revelation came by making efforts to conceal the incident, but often in such a way as to draw more attention. To shoot to kill was in a way understandable, part of a dirty war, but to lie that it had been done cast the operation as illicit, shameful – or else why lie, why not accept that a war required such violence? A whole series of revelations and denials, investigations and commissions, engendered a history of dirty tricks and a small library of articles, books, and television documentaries.

Soon after the 1974 bombs there were cases of British operations run into the Republic, operations that involved among other things the killing of IRA suspects by units and individuals operating along the border largely independently of central control. The fact that the security forces might be involved in all manner of dirty tricks in the six counties had been taken as a given by most republicans and an increasing number of nationalists. That the British would deny themselves an opportunity to direct operations within the Republic seemed unlikely to many, an increasing number as the years passed: even Jack Lynch had suspected the British in the 1972 bombs.

In time there were accusations and revelations of such British adventures. In October 1974, even before the Dublin bombs, an IRA volunteer, Eugene McQuaid, was killed by a booby-trapped rocket he was carrying on his bike at Dromada on the way from Dundalk to Newry. In January 1975 another IRA man, John Green, was shot and killed in a house in the Republic by cross-border raiders. Such incidents were grouped about what became known as the Nairac affair, after the British officer involved, Captain Robert Nairac, who was kidnapped and killed by the IRA in May 1977. Nairac, who was posthumously awarded a medal for valour, was not the only member of the British army along the border involved in covert operations.

There were other scandals over the years: a scandal over an RUC elite unit and the SAS charged with shooting and killing IRA suspects, a scandal over forcing men and women to inform, scandals over the purchase of evidence and the use of provocateurs. There were regular charges that the security forces and in particular British intelligence assisted and may perhaps at times have directed loyalists killer squads. Many nationalists believed the line between particular members of the Ulster Defence Regiment and the loyalist paramilitaries to be thin. In any case, year after year the dirty war generated reports of betrayal, intimidation, authorised murder – all ugly, all believed by some, some buttressed by real evidence and convincing data. Almost all were denied root and branch by security spokesmen.

Almost more revealing was the response to authorised investigations. The most famous was the inquiry by John Stalker into specific shoot-to-kill charges against the RUC. The long-running scandal over the eventual investigation by the Stalker Commission and the removal of Stalker on most dubious grounds simply extended the public life of the original cases. The Stalker affair, among others, indicated the ends to which the establishment would go to protect covert operations.

This was repeated and reinforced after each new revelation. In the case of the fall-out of the Gibraltar operation in March 1988, when the SAS were brought in and killed three unarmed IRA volunteers, it was not the killing but the coverage and response of the British establishment that focused attention on the illicit. Earlier a series of what became known as "supergrass" trials had already given an insight into the muddled underground war of informers, provocateurs, and handlers. There were from time to time revelations about those who carried out illegal and lethal operations while being handled. Gibraltar simply underlined the continuing British position on such matters: reveal nothing, deny everything, even the hard evidence.

Most important in eroding the British system's legitimacy was the long series of reversals and revelations following the trials of the Irish people convicted of setting off bombs in England. For years the convictions appeared sound, until at last investigation and new evidence managed to convince most that an injustice had been done. No matter about the evidence, the judicial system refused to admit error, an error that would put the system into doubt, a refusal that indeed put the system in doubt long before all the convictions in all the doubtful cases had proved unsound and the innocent were grudgingly released. Nearly everyone had accepted that there was very little justice for many within the Northern Ireland system – a means for the most part of putting suspected subversives and paramilitaries in prison; but increasingly British justice seemed impervious to both criticism and reform, mostly though not entirely in cases dealing with the Irish.

The cumulative effect of the body of evidence of violation of norms, of recourse to dirty tricks of one sort of another – from the actions of one British captain operating along the border up to the response of the entire British judicial system – created an atmosphere where the guilt of the British authorities could as easily be assumed as their innocence. There were the cases themselves, the informer evidence, the various cover-ups, the attitudes of the challenged establishment. There was also the recanting of several members of the British intelligence community: Peter Wright of MI5, Captain Colin Wallace and Captain Fred Holroyd, who had served in the British army in Northern Ireland, and Cathy Massiter. The first three published books, and Massiter appeared on television, to describe their experiences; and there were always the advocates of civil rights publishing further revelations. Critics were routinely damned and smeared as radicals, unsound romantics, or liars. The response often only created sympathy and a larger audience. There was as a result an audience ready to accept the improbable – often of course more than ready, eager and with limited interest in details, only in revelations that catered to old prejudices and political postures. Many in Ireland needed no further evidence, had never needed evidence of British perfidy or prejudice against the Irish; but even in Ireland many had felt these dirty tricks aberrant, the rules of fair play still valid. Time and the nature of the dirty war eroded these assumptions, and not only in Ireland.

Still the stereotype of the British as a fair, judicious and decent people now had competition. The British had often been accused of hypocrisy – never more often than by imperial rebels who had expected that the British would play by their own declared rules. But these little colonial wars had been far away and often soon over. Ireland was close by, under the eye of the media, and the Troubles went on and on. Thus, as the years passed, Irish events indicated that the authorities did not even play by the rules they kept rewriting. Such a judgement by old enemies was unfair, thought London, but not without visible evidence, thought others.

The Troubles had exacted a price that had not at first been visible in London, not recounted in the casualty figures of acceptable violence or the number of explosions but to be found in more elusive considerations. Faith in British justice had been eroded. The assumption of British fair play was no longer universal. There had been too many lies, too many self-confident, righteously indignant statements made by the authorities that soon proved to be not explanation but evasion.

The apparent loss of honour is a cost the arrogant can long pay with ease using capital accumulated by others. And whatever else, the English, certainly the establishment, have always been arrogant on Irish matters. London knows best, too often shows only intolerance and contempt for those who would not be like them and so accept them at their own estimation as exemplar and standard. Confusing the system with justice, the necessary with the right, criticism with treason, London over a generation in Ireland and so everywhere spent honour as easy coin. It is a cost that will have to be made good long after Ireland is not an issue. It has been a price not easy to weigh, but a real one.

Britain is no longer perceived, certainly not even in Anglophile Irish circles, as different in kind or degree from the other players in that dirty war. Since such wars concern perception – where winning or losing a hunger strike does not depend on survival, where the weak may humiliate the strong, lose their lives and win the day – then in this matter the British have lost a serious battle. They may have lost it for practical reasons, out of pride and loyalty to their own, out of contempt for those who would murder from a ditch, bomb innocent children, refuse concession much less co-option; but for whatever reason it has been lost – not all honour, of course, but enough to change the perception of those who observe Irish events.

What this meant was a rising level of analytical scepticism about the self-imposed limitations on British actions and the degree of toleration for the illicit within the British establishment. The British at some level, for whatever purpose, could have been responsible for the Dublin bombs of 1972, for the Dublin and Monaghan bombs of 1974; and if there was any evidence, however slight, to that effect, the British authorities almost certainly, as had been done in far less sensitive cases, would bring massive resources to bear in hiding any further revelations. The conclusion was, then, that the British authorities could have been involved, even in no-warning car bombs – not proved, still a matter of speculation, but as the years passed no longer beyond consideration.

As for the Government of the Republic, no one imagined for a moment that there had been collusion in the incidents; but just as the revelations of the Troubles had for Irish matters largely destroyed the credibility of the British establishment – certainly in Ireland – so too had the credibility of the Irish Government suffered. The actual problem was a gap between the historic positions that had for decades before the Northern events been little more than postures and the actual national interests. These interests, both of the people at large, as far as could be determined, and increasingly the Government, had become identical with those of the British. Peace and quiet were desired, with some honour left intact. Few in Dublin could any longer imagine a united Ireland, and many did not want one, did not want to pay for one, did not want the changes such an entity would bring. And fewer and fewer approved of the Provisional IRA's armed struggle and the threat to the stability and image of the Republic. All that was needed was a formula that would not be humiliating and would give a measure of security to Northern nationalists – no more.

At times the British establishment might not be aware of this convergence that brought Dublin and London together not just on visible matters like the Anglo-Irish Agreement of 1985 but on nearly all aspects of the Troubles. All that Dublin asked was that London understand the need for discretion. This was asking too much. Such realistic considerations, all to British advantage, were often ignored by British spokesmen and British politicians. The desires of the Irish played little part in repeated emotional responses to Irish events, and those events had little effect on cherished bias and convictions. The result was that the Government, whatever the composition, often appeared firmer on the national issue than was the case.

This meant that many observers assumed that the Government would go to some lengths to maintain the illusion that the historic ideals still held charm: after all, London certainly sounded at times as if this was the case, and the unionists and loyalists were so convinced. This was increasingly not the case. The historic aspirations were curtailed, the constitutional claims up for negotiation, the problems of the British authorities regarded with sympathy; and the Conservatives and the biased in London did not notice, if the Irish nationalists did. Governments in Dublin continually showed a willingness to co-operate publicly with the British. Only the contingent and unforeseen, like the hunger strikes, upset this response; and again all Dublin wanted was for the British to act with discretion, not arrogance. In time the paths met in November 1985 with the Anglo-Irish Agreement, but long before this the nature of the national issue had changed, and so the response to the British presence in Northern Ireland.

Thus even as early as 1974 or 1975 there might be reasons why the Government would be less than forthcoming on the bombs. Accusing the British was no way to bring the converging lines closer together, to forge a united front against gunmen. The Government, any Government, tolerated or encouraged British security intrusions, co-operated secretly with British security forces, sought the same subversives as the British. Why would Dublin want to embarrass London because of some erratic special operations, even one as deadly as that of May 1974? And, of course, Governments that had included all parties in 1972 and 1974 had not presided over a successful investigation of the bombing incidents. Perhaps they did not want to compound their difficulties with London? Perhaps there was a cover-up?

Since there was a remarkable lack of public hard data on the two bombing incidents, there was ample room for conspiracy theory, where lack of evidence becomes indicator, scattered evidence or disparate facts given coherence, and possibilities are taken as proved. In Ireland, then, many thought the British at some level were capable, directly or indirectly, of guiding the bombing operations, no matter who drove the cars. And after the events it was assumed that the British would deploy all manner of resource to hide either the reality or the possibility, and so of course there was no evidence. In Ireland, as well, many thought that any Government was capable of ignoring the incidents in the light of policy needs and so refusing to examine the distant past for fear of discovering an unpleasant reality. And of course there would be no evidence of doing nothing. Thus lack of evidence encouraged speculation and assumptions about the bombing incidents.

These assumptions, stated and unstated, were common currency by the time a re-evaluation of the 1974 bombs began in a most unlikely quarter. Colonel John Morgan, former Director of Intelligence of the Defence Forces, was concerned not only with the seeming military nature of the 1974 bombs but also with the families of the victims who had been forgotten, were without memorial. On examining the events of May 1974 he felt that the visible structure of the operation was shaped by a military hand: the results were those that would have occurred had the British army been in charge. From there he sought hard evidence.

Morgan was a private citizen, not a private detective, not an investigative journalist or a trained historian. He had no appropriate experience and no resources. He did have time, determination, enthusiasm, and persistence. He found others. Some of those who expressed interest were alienated by the establishment. Some had formed the 1968 Committee to stress that many matters had not changed in twenty years – certainly nothing had been done about the 1974 bombs. Some of those concerned were suspected of subversive leanings by those they criticised. Many were discounted as marginal by the authorities: what did someone like Kevin Boland, a lone and ignored voice since the Arms Trial, have to offer twenty years later? No matter, the logic of doing something for the relatives attracted others to the case or to the need for a formal memorial. The 1974 bombs re-emerged from the past still a mystery, still a painful matter. And Colonel Morgan kept to his rounds, seeking data and logic where little was to be found.

Morgan generated a revived concern about the victims' families that at last led to recognition of the dead. At noon on 17 May 1992, a monument to the victims was unveiled in Parnell Square near the Garden of Remembrance and a wreath placed by Kevin Boland. There was a reception for the relatives at the Gresham Hotel in O'Connell Street. In the evening there was a memorial Mass at the Pro-Cathedral in Dublin in commemoration of the victims under the auspices of the 1968 Committee. The famous and important did not attend this ceremony as they had the first one in May 1974. At least something, however, had been done, arising from Morgan's concern; the victims and their families had not been forgotten. The survivors had not yet attracted the concern of the authorities, those implicitly criticised for forgetting the victims and forgoing a continuing search for the bombers.

In May 1994, President Mary Robinson attended when the memorial had been moved to a site off Cathal Brugha Street but still nothing had come from the Gardaí.

The search for the 1974 bombers had not been a simple matter at the time, and obviously the prospects when Morgan arrived on the scene were even less promising. His conviction that the operation was what a military planner would do could be fed with very limited hard data. Ultimately, his speculation about the military structure of the bombing operation led him to a meeting with a British documentary producer, Glyn Middleton of Yorkshire Television. To Morgan's conviction were added the determination, drive and skills of the Yorkshire group of Middleton and Mark Ackerman, who decided to do a film on the forgotten massacre.

The Yorkshire Television people, their contacts and researchers sought evidence of British involvement. Suspects were hunted down and questioned, trails were uncovered, and probably some avenues closed off. In a country filled with rumour, speculation and recollections clouded by the passage of time, this investigation was no easy matter. All sorts of gossip and suggestions were traced to source and found wanting. Enormous effort was spent trying to prove that the safe haven after the bomb was a house in Kildare, and at the end there was the word of a reliable IRA volunteer, long dead, given to others and ignored because IRA headquarters did not want the Gardaí rummaging through Kildare where the Provos had arms dumps. So in the end the threads ran out, could not even be mentioned, one strand lost by lack of data and another frayed, most strands lost.

Most startlingly, the Gardaí for the first time revealed what they knew – details that made revelations enough for the producers. As for the rest, enough was left to weave an intriguing if not always convincing programme. The result was "The Hidden Hand: the Forgotten Massacre", which was broadcast on 6 July 1993 on Independent Television. It was a documentary that could be seen only in the part of Ireland reached by Ulster Television or cable television because of RTE's refusal to transmit the programme. The partial showing only added to the controversy generated by the implications of the documentary.

The most unexpected aspects arose from the Garda information. In effect, Yorkshire Television had persuaded members of the Gardaí to read but not hand over the results of the official investigation in 1974 and 1975. This investigation – still formally open – had implicated by name some twenty loyalists, eight of these from eye-witness reports. Obviously some in the Gardaí had long memories of what had seemed a betrayal of their efforts, in that no Government attempt had been made to seek appropriate co-operation from the authorities in Northern Ireland. The point had been made: the Gardaí had found the perpetrators and had been thwarted somehow by someone, for purposes unknown.

To the details of the loyalist involvement, convincing and seemingly damaging to all those in responsibility in Dublin in 1974 and 1975, the programme's producers presented a case for British involvement that was circumstantial and conjectural, capable of convincing those who had long suspected such British dirty tricks but less convincing to the sceptical, a case made on speculation, assumptions, and reconstruction. Unlike the loyalist presence, in the end the British involvement was not proved, nor was it clear that anyone in Dublin had intentionally closed down the investigation.

The British response to the programme was, as tended to be the case with Irish matters in 1993, tepid. Those in power saw no reason to discuss journalistic speculation. The Irish Troubles had produced a long series of television revelations, and the Conservative government could do without one more such exercise. It was not even a nine-day wonder, barely rippled British political waters, and drew only routine denials. It might be good television but there was no case to answer, at least not in Belfast and London: the Irish had never asked about the UVF, and there was no evidence of any involvement of the security forces – mere speculation.

In Ireland it was another matter, since the hard data concerned the case in Garda hands and the responsibilities of the Government of the time. The revelations and speculations of the programme produced a variety of responses and statements, except for the then Taoiseach, Liam Cosgrave, who made it a practice to make no comment on the past. Some of these responses were not so much economical with the truth as irrelevant to the issues. It was not that lies were told but rather that the truth of the matter was not clear.

What was important was not what had occurred but what had not occurred, and who, if anyone, was responsible for the UVF suspects not being pursued by formal means. As for the Government of the time, any British involvement was then, as it was after the Yorkshire programme, a matter of speculation.

It was the Garda evidence given to Yorkshire Television that caused a fuss. Essentially some in the Gardaí in 1993 wanted it made clear that the evidence of the identity of the perpetrators was not really evidence, since it would not stand up in court. The suspects had not been in an identity parade before the eye-witnesses, and so had not been identified. The suspects had not been questioned, could not be questioned without permission. The RUC had questioned none of them. No one had followed up. No one in Dublin had formally approached the Northern Ireland Office or the RUC or anyone else in Northern Ireland to permit the investigation to be pursued. Those involved in the Department of Justice, the Security Committee and the Government of the time insisted that no one had told them of the UVF identifications. There was thus nothing for them to do.

The reason seemed to be that somewhere as the data moved up towards the top of the Gardaí it became apparent that there was not a strong enough case to put before the Government. And none within that Government – for whatever reason – was demanding progress. The Government then had not suppressed anything, even had it been capable of wishing to do so, because nothing came formally to the attention of those responsible. The Minister for Justice, Patrick Cooney, noted that the Gardaí might have been discussing names but that nothing came before him. As the Minister for Defence of the time, Patrick Donegan, said, no list was brought by the Gardaí to the Security Committee or the Government; and, he added, in retrospect he very much doubted that the British army was involved in the planting of the bombs.

Conor Cruise O'Brien too recalled that the Gardaí had not reported any lack of co-operation on the part of the RUC, for if they had, Garret FitzGerald as Minister for Foreign Affairs would have been able to raise it through proper channels with the Northern Secretary, Merlyn Rees. Justin Keating, then in the Government as Minister for Industry and Commerce, indicated that if the matter had come before the Government it would, he felt sure, have taken a serious view of the RUC sitting on the investigation.

Individually and collectively, those involved who made statements indicated that neither the lack of RUC co-operation nor the existence of specific suspects had reached the political figures responsible. Twenty years later all those responsible resented being accused of collusion or a cover-up. What was really being asked of the Government of the day was why someone responsible had not shown more urgency, simply shown more curiosity. Why had the Garda Commissioner not been asked for details? Why had the Commissioner not simply offered more details? None of those responsible in the Government replied to this line of questioning but merely pointed to the record: nothing had crossed their desks.

In a small country investigating the greatest crime in its history, apparently none of those responsible, formally at least, had asked at any time if there were suspects or if there was ample or any co-operation over the border. The Government seemed content to accept whatever was given without question, and the senior Garda people seemed reticent to detail their progress. Not having a case ready for court, they said nothing.

Wittingly or unwittingly, consciously or not, those involved lacked a sense of urgency that might have revealed the UVF suspects and the obstruction of the Northern authorities. At the time, the media and the public and most observers without recourse to Garda data assumed that loyalists had been responsible. Apparently no one in the Government was curious enough to ask the Gardaí about this assumption, certainly to ask so that an answer would be on the record. And the Gardaí felt no pressure to produce answers – apparently the reverse. All this is interesting, indicative of the nature and priorities of the Government of the day, but was not in any conventional sense a cover-up.

Even if the data had reached the Government or the public the result seemingly would have been little different from similar revelations concerning British operations. If the UVF had contacts, these would not be revealed, and if they had no contacts then there was nothing to be revealed. On the matter of the Dublin bombs in 1974 many, nearly all, of the loyalists were assumed to have too much knowledge of Ulster dirty tricks to allow them to go before the media and the public, to allow them to make an appearance in any formal setting. Several of the UVF people were then on British payrolls. Others had been used before. The British would plead "operational needs" in public and devise a strategy of plausible denial, even if there were no British connection with the bombing operations.

The Gardaí must have known this. Later John Stalker would discover in a less contentious case that revelations about covert operations were so unwelcome that those in London would go to most lengths to see that buried bones stayed interned. Yet at the time the scope of the atrocity of May 1974 was so great that few observers would have imagined that the case would die out within the Gardaí rather than emerging in public for at least cathartic purposes.

In 1993 many in the Republic were not content to have the incidents reburied; the interest and concern did not just evaporate. On Monday 13 September, Dublin County Council called for a sworn inquiry to investigate the 1974 bombs. The councillors were concerned not only with Garda failures but collusion with the RUC and of course the alleged assistance given to the UVF by British intelligence. The public as well as the councillors wanted the conspiracy to have a proper ending, the guilty at least known and the threads tied up. Instead the television programme had merely presented more questions, more possibilities, hidden some names but revealed more possibilities. More important, the programme generated new concern about whose hands had really been behind the massacre.

Twenty years after the event the Yorkshire documentary remains largely speculation, the origin of the bombing operation uncertain, the details beyond those known in 1974 to the Gardaí hidden and likely to stay so. And much the same is true for 1972–73, where the public data is even more scanty. For recognised states, secret wars are best kept secret, and deviations from the conventional must be denied, however implausible the denial.

Plausible denial is in fact the price the secret state pays to justice and decency. And in their arrogance most states do not even bother to be very plausible about operations run for the sake of national security. Public denial and outraged indignation are usually deemed ample, and so honour is salvaged. This is not exactly so. There is no honour for those who dare to win by illicit means, no matter how alluring such a victory or how vile the opponent. And so the bombs of Dublin and Monaghan, the bombs of 1972, 1973, and 1974, have handlers but no parents.

Chapter VIII

The Dublin bombs, if without parents, were not without reason. Such bombs in 1972 and 1974 should not have been unexpected. The Troubles could not be pent up within six counties, for in theory and in fact both the Republic and Britain were arena as well to a multi-dimensional Anglo-Irish unconventional conflict. This struggle could not be contained by legal definitions, analytical categories, or wishful thinking. The Dublin and Monaghan bombs were in fact not the only bombs detonated in the Republic nor the only violence that came south. There had been other incidents, especially in the spill-over of the violence along the border, but even in Dublin.

There would never be any perpetrators caught and sentenced for most of the violence in the Republic. There would rarely indeed be any suspects as certain as the bombers from the mid-Ulster UVF in 1974 nor as likely as those who drove the cars south in 1972. Most of the other bombs had no suspects, some had no rationale, just bombs without specific cause and without discernible effect, signs of the times. And there would be killings without bombs, murder using the Republic as arena.

A man would be killed in an attempt to bomb Official Sinn Féin's hired train on the way to Bodenstown. The Wolfe Tone monument at the north-east corner of St Stephen's Green, Dublin, no aesthetic joy, would survive a loyalist explosive device. Dublin would pass uneasily through a spate of small bombs, though not so small in that the foyer of the Shelbourne Hotel was turned into rubble on 13 February 1976. These were planted by Belfast rogue Provos, without warning and without authority and certainly without rationale beyond ill-directed spite and malice. There would be other mini-bombs and arson devices in the city. The loyalist paramilitaries from time to time, without great planning and with limited explanations, would penetrate into alien territory to deposit their primitive fireworks, a sporting event for the bored defenders.

The most provocative intrusions were, as the authorities had always feared, those of the republicans. The Provisional IRA Army Council could always find compelling reasons to ignore Army Order no. 8 and authorise operations in the twenty-six counties. It was war, and sometimes the target was too tempting, or money was needed, or the locals acted spontaneously. On 21 July 1976 the British ambassador, Christopher Ewart-Biggs, was assassinated with a mine in a culvert that detonated under his car just beyond his residence in Sandyford, County Dublin. The IRA operations officer had noted the ambassador's intelligence background – and his vulnerability – and the chief of staff had authorised a special active service unit. When the INLA emerged, they had no compunction about operating in the Republic. It was easy to bring the war into the Republic, and difficult to keep it out for everyone involved.

Over the years the more obvious republican operations tended to be armed bank raids by the Provisionals, by the supposedly defunct Officials, and by the INLA. The Provos were supposedly limited to attempts that would return substantial sums, but these often turned out to be smash-and-grab raids by armed men with limited vision and capacity breaking into a rural post office. There were authorised IRA kidnappings – one that led to the murder of a Garda. Some even suspected, not without reason, that the loss of the racehorse Shergar, snatched and hidden and never found, could be laid at the door of a prominent, almost retired IRA man with experience in the horse trade.

And there were those with almost no political connections who used the republican banner as a flag of convenience for armed robberies or kidnapping or whatever offered a profit and could be claimed a political deed, steal for the republic and spend the returns. And this led to shoot-outs at roadblocks or in the middle of towns.

It was this creeping violence that alarmed many in Dublin

who wanted the Republic to be, as far as possible, isolated from the Provos' armed struggle, who wanted as many of the Provos as possible behind bars. Everyone was still fearful too that the loyalists would be provoked and come south again into Dublin, as they had in 1972 and 1974. In fact this response continued to give the loyalists the rationale for just such intrusions: Dublin claimed the Provos provoked trouble, and so too did the loyalists; Dublin would only get what Dublin deserved.

It was as much as anything the loyalist perception of Dublin as centre of their own troubles that worried the authorities, for they realised that the UVF and UDA saw no difference between the IRA and themselves, the Government, the Irish establishment, nationalists, everyone in the Republic. What tended to protect the Republic in general and Dublin in particular from the loyalist paramilitaries was not governmental attitudes or statements or restraint by the IRA, or even events in Northern Ireland, but loyalist perceptions. The defenders felt that the Dublin centre was far away, alien and strange, protected by Rome and distance and hostile nationalists.

It was this conviction of the fundamentalists, men of limited education and narrow perspectives, that tended to protect Dublin. The city, so different from Belfast, was embedded in a countryside that to loyalist eyes was enemy territory, so strange as to be rarely even tempting. The loyalist paramilitary was a defender, not a rebel, a man for the system, not one to go far to find targets. Thus, for the loyalist paramilitaries, if they were involved in 1972 and as they most certainly were in 1974, the most significant ingredient for a Dublin operation was not the infusion of skill and talent, training or detonators, plans and options, but the very idea of such an intrusion. The Dublin bombs required a stretch of imagination by those not noted for imagination, highly conservative killers who targeted tomorrow the same prey that had served yesterday. This is why the bombs in Dublin were so special.

The IRA planned as easily for Gibraltar or the Netherlands as for Belfast; after all, a century earlier the Fenians had invaded Canada several times, and England was always a potential battle arena. Their target was the power of the Crown, the forces that oppressed Ireland. The loyalists sought rather to hold their territory, so hard won in blood, so long defended against internal and external enemies, so long at risk of betrayal. They feared not only the dream of the republicans but also the limits of their own dream, a matter of tactic, not an inch, the past as the future, and the potential for betrayal of the union by its very advocates in London.

Unattractive in theory, unappealing in explanation and posture, denied by the contemporary world, isolated, misunderstood, object of media scorn and international calumny, the loyalists hunkered down in the redoubt of their traditions, amid the safety found along the Shankill Road or the hill farms of Antrim or Armagh. There they lived with like, and the Union Jack flew. There the patriotic commemorations were marked, the symbols revered, and the rituals kept. This that they held they would defend. They sought not the whole country, not a nation, but a security too often denied a chosen people.

The UVF had no compunction about killing the Miami Showband – Irish, Catholic, and so up to no good. The very presence in Armagh of the minibus was ample provocation. To go south across the border, to move among others was another matter. Such ventures were not often on an agenda. To bomb Dublin required an adjustment of perception, not an easy matter for defenders, parochial and strong in habits; that sort of march could not easily be set to Lambeg drums.

Such an operation, a 1972 or a 1974 bombing, had its attraction, of course, but only if construed as appropriate. This could most easily be accomplished by suggestion from the articulate. Defenders might thus be co-opted by those with longer views or might even be inspired by the example of the bold, as may well have happened with the January 1973 bomb. Thus the first penetration, the first expedition, had to be more closely shaped by those with a greater purpose and experience with tactical flexibility as well as familiarity with organisation, even with access to material: those within the security forces at some level, at various levels, who in discussion and surely in deeds in 1972 shaped an operation that could be swiftly mounted, that could be easily denied, and – given the assumptions of the involved and the spirit of the time – that would be highly effective for political purposes.

The logic of the 1972 bombs in November and December was not that of the defenders, but the January 1973 Dublin bomb and those of 1974 had a certain follow-on loyalist logic. All it would really take was a few conversations over a pint and at most a box or two of gear along with the nod of authorisation from a treasured ally; mind you, I've said nothing.

The UVF might undertake such an operation with less guidance and more enthusiasm, second time easy; but the very idea of penetration into the nationalist heartland before 1972 seldom lasted beyond the pub. And if less true after the Dublin bombs of 1972, still operations in the Republic – except along the border, in close association with covert operators – remained for a generation rare and so problematical. The assumption is that any spectacular or effective effort arose not from the councils of the UVF in Portadown or the Shankill, both content to operate within the murder triangle or along the Belfast fault lines, but from the perceived needs and fantasies of some in the security forces.

The loyalists might later bomb symbols at Bodenstown or in St Stephen's Green or leave devices in department stores. Such incidents could be organised quickly by two or three defenders without great risk or resources. The need to retaliate in response to Provo or INLA provocation and the pressure to take action against the blatant nationalists could best and most swiftly be answered within Northern Ireland. There at home there was less need for skill and talent, less need even for daring. There the will and the capacity to rationalise sectarian murder as a legitimate defence for a generation proved ample, and so cross-border operations, large or small, were rare.

If cross-border operations by loyalists were rare, if the technical and managerial talents for undertaking such operations were scanty in loyalist circles, then, many observers agree, the British must have played a decisive role, however that role was structured. No-one can see the RUC so involved, and nearly everyone imagines that those attached to the vague intelligence-military groups hidden away off the bureaucratic chart must be the key.

Yet there is a lack of hard data. The 1972 bombs appeared to lead to names associated with the British security forces; even this was lacking in the 1974 bombs. And the operations of 1972 and 1974 that have seemed so elaborate to the military mind were not beyond loyalist capacities. Regular soldiers are prone to forget the blunders of battle, the haphazard nature of war, and the ingenuity of those without training in military academies. Part of the time the Provisional IRA are regarded as bumbling Paddies but at other times are transmuted into professional terrorists, if for no other reason than to give rationale for security failures and security budgets. That the British army would require time, planning, a great many people and the exchange of considerable paper to set the Dublin bombs does not mean that others would be so constrained: the IRA managed to mortar Downing Street and to put the entire British government at risk in Brighton without moving paper or attending mid-career seminars. The loyalists might be crude of nature, ruthless and without educational certification, but their unconventional general strike brought down the new Executive, and so why could those less dedicated to political action not bring a few car bombs to Dublin?

Simply because those car bombs in 1972 and 1974 were so lethal, so effective, and because no one was caught, there was among professionals and observers the feeling that someone with qualifications must be involved, someone with conventional skills. There were, therefore, rumours, asides to published revelations, hints and guesses about who the puppet-master might be; but most of the "evidence" arose from logical arguments and reasonable assumptions, not from data, not from the eye-witnesses of 1974 or the car hire records of 1972.

The lack of very much hard data about British covert actions in Ireland is hardly a matter of chance. A great deal of care, trouble, intimidation and influence has been expended to keep

British secrets secret. In this the British intelligence establishment and their political associates are hardly alone: state secrets must be kept, if not at all costs then at great cost. Only when the cover is lifted by violence or by error are operations revealed; and even then it is rare to discover what went before or after. Even long afterwards, those who keep the secrets do not want scholars rummaging through fifty-year-old files or elderly officers writing their memoirs. Only the collapse of all order, the disappearance of a regime and so of the guardians of the files leads to extensive revelations, as with Nazi Germany and Fascist Italy and more recently to a degree with the members of the Warsaw Pact; and even there files were closed again as fast as possible to keep potential assets in place for the next generation.

In Northern Ireland during the last twenty-five years a single constant has been the enormous effort the British have put into maintaining cover, regularly discounting or discrediting revelations: even those by minor figures, even those on the margins of events. The tribulations of Fred Holroyd and Colin Wallace, once involved in intelligence and dirty tricks and later in revealing the details, were not all imagined. There were also the highly public efforts to prevent the publication of Peter Wright's *Spycatcher*, efforts far out of proportion to the revelations of an embittered crank living out retirement in the outback. The pressures, often in public, exerted by the British establishment on the media or on anyone probing intelligence matters have seldom been subtle.

Most of the revelations on Ireland have come from the left or from those easily categorised as nationalists – both suspect, both out to damage the system. Only a few from within the system have emerged. And neither the extensive trials nor the experience of the co-opted and intimidated have produced much of a body of evidence. The resources of the British government to restrict revelation have been available across an entire spectrum of assets: money, force, loyalty, greed, disinformation, the law, patriotism, fear – all have been deployed for the Crown. All at one time or another have been used to protect the covert, to punish investigation, to maintain plausible denial, and often long past reason: the Gibraltar case, the Stalker case, any case focused on the covert. And if in the end nothing works, then firm denial, regardless of the evidence. And for a generation the British security forces have largely kept their secrets, given the nature of an open society, a curious press, and, in Ireland, a suspicious arena.

It is thus no great surprise that the responsibility for the Dublin bombs has had to remain speculative. There was limited if real initial assistance from the authorities in Northern Ireland, or at least from the RUC. Once secrets were suspected within the security establishment, such co-operation ended; the RUC had to give up any pretence of disinterested concern. Nothing was to be gained by saying anything, and so cover was maintained. Perhaps there was nothing to cover, but who wanted to discover this was not the case?

What is also covered, hidden by denial or evasion, is the little-understood fact that such special operations, successful or not, often remain elusive. These affairs rarely have a neat beginning or an easily-discovered end. They are cut by need to know, hidden by self-denial, clouded by perception and perspective, and blurred during the building of plausible denial. In many such operations no one is ever responsible: no Soldier B with a smoking gun who has made a decision with all the facts. No one even has all the facts – certainly not Soldier B with the gun – and so no one has responsibility for the result. There is no single guiding hand, no guilty ministers in Westminster or responsible secretary in Whitehall. Yet no captain operating along the border can run free for long, kill for pleasure or profit or political purpose, without those in distant offices playing some part. Gibraltar led to Downing Street, and, many felt, so must the Dublin bombs, no matter than Downing Street knew nothing.

The orders and understandings passed down to that Soldier B are gradually shaped to murder within the rules, murder denied, murder equipped with explanation, and no one person to blame, certainly not Soldier B who pulled the trigger. Downing Street, Westminster, Whitehall, the Northern Ireland Office, the British army and the RUC are all permeated with attitudes and assumptions and so acquiescence. Everyone is responsible, and no one: not a godfather of violence but an extended family.

That is the nature of dirty tricks in Ireland, at best acts of war in peace and at worst criminal folly disguised as military action. Such operations must always be deniable, ever secret, and are often lethal as well as foolish. But most important of all, they are immune to orderly analysis.

Those who would have the plain tale of events in 1974 have most often suspected that the British in some manner directed the operation for limited political purpose at a time of great tension – a rerun of 1972. And they have suspected that at worst the Irish Government tolerated the exercise if it did not collude in the cover-up. Everyone accepted without much data the fact that the loyalists were the actual perpetrators; in 1972 some felt that those directly involved were in or attached to British intelligence. All the hard data there is is what came from the Garda leak in the *Evening Herald* in 1973. As for 1974, in twenty years, as a result of the Yorkshire Television investigation, the only convincing hard information that has been uncovered is the UVF mid-Ulster connection. All else related to 1974 is speculation, circumstantial, unproved, and to those who require convincing, unconvincing.

Certainly in retrospect the most curious aspect of the May 1974 bombs was the apparent lack of official urgency at the higher levels of government. The Dublin and Monaghan spectacular was the greatest, most lethal crime in the history of Ireland and Britain, and yet those in London, Belfast and Dublin showed a remarkable lack of curiosity about the perpetrators. There were then and later ample explanations for the lack of concern and so lack of involvement in the developing case, for the lack of pressure in Dublin. There was a similar lack of interest in Northern Ireland and Britain, but for other reasons.

Responses to such matters as the 1974 bombs always follow certain bureaucratic courses in Ireland. Such events were handled properly at each level. Such crimes were not the currency of Government discussion or even ministerial management.

Matters had been pursued properly and judiciously and had not led then or since to a conclusion that would require further involvement.

All this was true. Yet after the greatest crime in the history of the state, after the bodies were strewn on the Dublin and Monaghan streets, the country appalled, the people devastated, none within the central circle seemed to have asked formally who was responsible. None pursued the matter with the Gardaí, formally or informally. Ireland is a small country and the Dublin establishment smaller yet. The Gardaí felt that the higher they went with their findings and suspicions the less enthusiasm there was. Yet those at the higher levels insisted that the findings were inadequate to require further action, and at the top no one asked who was suspected, who was thought responsible, what the investigators knew. The Gardaí involved in the investigation knew that further aid from the RUC was dependent upon formal channels being opened within the Dublin establishment, and somewhere between the evidence about the UVF and the decision to seek higher authority the case evaporated.

There are always good bureaucratic and procedural reasons for doing nothing, letting matters take their course. And the Government had many pressing priorities. There was no standard operating procedure in such matters, no recognised duty to be done. There were certainly political reasons for not pursuing matters if the British intelligence agencies, the British army or the RUC were to be found to be involved. It was, the Government felt, bad enough that the Northern Ireland Office in the midst of the general strike was willing to talk to loyalist leaders whose organisations must have been involved in the bombing. None in the Government, however, had officially asked the Gardaí if this indeed was the case. And so they had not been told.

Even in 1974 some thought that, as in 1972, the bombers had not acted alone. It was not be the first time such suspicions had arisen in public from data that could not convince a court. In 1974 as the months passed, no one of prominence suggested that this might be the case for the Dublin and Monaghan bombs and nearly twenty years later those who had said nothing then still felt that there was nothing to say: there was no evidence that the British were involved, only the loyalists; and Yorkshire Television had not proved otherwise.

Perhaps no one in Dublin wanted to discover British involvement in 1974. If this were the case, all sorts of matters might surface. The Gardaí had contacts with both the RUC and the British army, and both the RUC and British army had been involved in dubious pursuits, pursuits that those in authority in Belfast and London might disclaim but if proved would greatly complicate any future political accommodation. None in Dublin would collude at hiding evidence, but few in the Government wanted to believe, then or later, that the British could have been involved. The informed knew that British intelligence was deeply involved in loyalist paramilitary activities. It was hardly impossible that some of these handlers had been privy to the operation if not the guiding force.

If the British had allowed their agents such free play, they were fools or at least foolish; but then, the British had often been foolish in Irish matters. And perhaps those in charge at the Northern Ireland Office knew as little as the Irish Government – certainly wanted to find no evidence of scandal, so also asked no questions. Another scandal would be to no one's advantage. So why seek evidence, cause trouble, complicate a future that would depend on Anglo-Irish amity?

The collapse of the Northern Ireland Assembly and so the Council of Ireland, the best feasible accommodation Dublin could imagine, could not be repaired by building on an accusation from Dublin of authorised murder. No one in authority in Ireland need articulate such considerations. Perhaps no one did. Perhaps no one considered the possibility. In any case no one said anything, then or later, but waited for the system to run its course. So the investigation wound its way through channels, found indicators but not evidence, data but not proof. Unless there was real proof no one need take action, and in the meantime no one need ask anything.

All could be assured, if thought were given, that in such

matters real evidence rarely appears and so rarely need be found on a ministerial desk. None would hinder the investigation of murder, and all wanted justice done; but if this were not possible, then no purpose could be served by giving the authority of the state to unwarranted suspicions. What purpose would such suspicion serve but to be divisive? Those at the top of the Gardaí hardly expected the RUC or the British army to be more co-operative. To pursue the matter once the sources had dried up would be to cause trouble unnecessarily. Justice would be no better served and the necessary accommodation in the North delayed.

So sensible men did no more than their duty. The system ran by the book, and the case was unresolved, the suspects' guilt not proved. The Gardaí involved were moved on to other matters, some bitter, some with resignation. And the passage of time eroded the last bit of urgency and finally even much of the memory of the bombs.

The victims and the survivors were forgotten. The bombs of 1974, like those of 1972 and 1973, became part of a past filled with horrors best forgotten.

When Yorkshire Television arrived, members of the Gardaí broke the long silence and, on a case still technically open, read details of the UVF involvement – names, dates, places, eye-witnesses – to the English producers. It was a one-time affair, and subsequent requests were denied. In fact the case was reactivated as a result of the television programme, although no progress was reported, no task force named, no further statement given. Only the most cynical, however, suspect that there was any Irish collusion, any Government or Garda cover-up, but rather at most a certain lethargy that allowed political matters to proceed without scandal – hardly a crime and hardly even a conscious decision.

Over the years much of the country grew cynical about the covert activities of the British security forces, which at times seemed to have authority on the highest level to wage secret war. Certainly the covert operators were not always so covert, were repeatedly caught or involved in the more unsavoury aspects of the dirty war. These intrusions into the underground at least had a certain legitimacy; the failings and horrors of the paramilitaries, the intentional sectarian murders of the loyalists, the blunders by bombers and marksmen that contaminated the Provos' crusade, the rationalisations and recrimination of invisible gunmen, did not. They were the sordid underside of self-proclaimed defenders and liberators. All these secret armies and covert defenders were unofficial, illicit, killed for a cause; if one imperfectly understood and often badly served. The forces of the Crown, however, were held to other standards. Their dirty tricks seemed especially unpleasant because they were deployed by the legitimate.

If the security forces were legitimate, they at times still acted in alignment with their loyalist associates. Dublin might not be involved in collusion, but the British were another matter. What was legitimate was no longer quite clear. Running a killer was much the same as killing.

Simply because the British were legitimate, they had many defenders, could count on excuses, toleration, and the cover of the system. And, most important, the no-warning killings, the corruption of justice, the bizarre special operations, the public lies and private brutality could be excused by damning the critics as traditional enemies: republican apologists, leftist loonies, Irish nationalists. So no matter how blatant the violation of the rules, the critics were discounted by the British establishment. Such critics were involved in propaganda exercises about events that if real were in any case necessary, reactions that were provoked by the far greater horrors visited by the IRA. If the critics arose from within the system they were damned as unstable and disgruntled, giving aid and comfort to the enemy. And so too the media, only eager for scandal and novelty, not part of the team, also a comfort to the enemy.

The main enemy, and for good reason, was always the IRA. And those who would restrict the security forces, insist on peace rules even during the war against terrorism, were apologists for the murder of innocents, advocates of subversion, weak and impractical, treasonous more likely. The British people did not want their army slandered, abhorred the IRA who set no-warning bombs in English cities, were, Labour or Conservative, more often delighted at effective military response than alarmed at civil rights violations.

And in Dublin there was no official sympathy for many of the victims of such British actions. Increasingly the Provos were seen as mad dogs, subversives who should be put down, gunmen who tainted the image of the new Ireland. Even the rituals and displays of nationalism became muted, past gunmen no longer such heroes, old grievances no longer so pressing, a united Ireland no longer a desirable necessity. All Dublin wanted was an end to the Troubles, an end to the Provos' campaign. The establishment simply wanted the British authorities to use discretion and to deny themselves if possible recourse to the unconventional so that the sleeping resentments of Irish nationalism would not be awakened. Surely the British, so powerful, so publicly dedicated to law and fair play, might deny recourse to the illicit and covert?

Several factors over the years made such a denial unappealing to those involved. First there was pressure for action from those at risk – and these targets ran from the part-time police constable to the Prime Minister and included at times even those who had said the harsh word about the Provos or the wrong one to the authorities. Those in the firing line had a toleration of hard but effective methods. Second, those who sought a mandate for such methods often were not so much authorised as tolerated: plausible denial did not become hard-edged at one point in the bureaucratic chain, but responsibility eroded in proportion to the distance from the act. A shoot-to-kill policy that murdered suspects, too often the wrong suspects, too often publicly, was not decided around a table and noted in minutes but evolved from the pressures in the field. What was needed was a sense of the possible and the enthusiasm for action by those at the point. Things that could be done were often done because they could be done. There were nods and winks and assumptions made about the removal of troublesome gunmen or arrogant subversives.

The British government's unconventional operations were often not so much unorthodox in practice as in authorisation: no one was responsible. And over time the nature of British dirty tricks became far more a given than had been the case in 1974 or 1972. The system was addicted to the covert, unashamed of the illicit.

And so for the critics, everyone in the system, in the chain of command, was responsible: Margaret Thatcher was as guilty of the shooting of the three IRA volunteers in Gibraltar in March 1988 as were those who stalled the investigation, those who adjusted the rules to secrecy's advantage, those who lied in public, not to mention those who on someone's orders were allowed to pull the trigger, were prepared for the kill by standard orders and so did kill. Few critics understood the system, the codes and texts of authority or the sophistication of evasion that a special language and special practice permits, encourages. Everyone understood that dirty tricks had become endemic in Irish matters.

Books were written heaping all operations on the heads of the SAS or depicting a vast, mechanical bureaucracy of highly trained operatives eager to adjust the rules to the needs of the moment. Even when the evidence proved convincing to the disinterested, the tone of the accusation, the politics of the accuser, the defence by the British government and its friends tended to deflect the attack. Despite all this, despite all the advantages of the state and the blunders of the Provos and the loyalists, as the years passed and the Troubles ground on in a lethal stalemate, the evidence of British dirty tricks accumulated, could not be wished away.

A dirty war had – and had from the first – lured the authorities into special operations. Some operations, of course, went as planned, stayed secret, and encouraged the rest. Yet when revealed, these operations almost always embarrassed the government and amazed observers at the folly of those involved: the arrogance, the assumption that cover is inviolate, that to be ruthless is to be pragmatic, that terror can without cost be deployed against terrorists, even against their advocates.

All the British intelligence agencies had run those without qualification or skills, only the capacity for the main chance. All the special units, under varying names, had tolerated or encouraged individuals to take risks, violate norms, handle the unsavoury, even kill without guidelines or supervision. Relations with the loyalist paramilitaries were ambivalent: the UVF or the UDA saw themselves as always in alliance with their army, as they pursued mutual goals. They felt they were allies, not creatures, even when paid. The British tended to assume such a defender to be a malleable instrument of his handler, a paid pawn. For the British the subtleties of Ireland had to be learned and relearned as tours ended and the actors changed, and many so involved brought only bias and ambition to the task. If, as time passed, those involved grew more subtle, so did their opponents, and the real world of Ireland more complex. All the blunders could not be buried, the scandals hidden, the loyalist connections convincingly denied, the lethal operations kept covered.

What was impressive over a generation was that so much was hidden, so much kept beyond the media or the public, so much not lied away but never revealed. At times over the years nothing helped those who would keep the secret war a secret, and so the watchers accumulated a dossier on British covert acts beyond easy rationalisation. The bounds of British unconventional forays proved porous, flexible, hardly a restraint.

The Secret Intelligence Service (MI6), eager to compete with the Security Service (MI5), despatched as agents not only their own but also often anyone passably plausible. MI5 competed not only with MI6 but also with British army intelligence, in turn often compartmentalised into competing units. None of the British quite trusted the Irish, no matter how loyal, and so mistrusted the RUC, while the RUC in turn often found their British colleagues as troublesome as the opposition. All of this added to the very nature of covert operations, and produced almost routinely the scandals that so enraged observers and victims.

What the British were soon caught at in Northern Ireland was regular recourse to irregular tactics, in violation of the norms of Britain, the Northern Ireland Office, and the security forces. There were trap ambushes, provocateurs, purchased terrorists, toleration and encouragement of crime and criminals, and, if all else failed, the deployment of their own for illicit operations. It was possible to believe the worst. No one could prove, for example, that a bomb placed near the Alliance Party's office in Belfast during the election campaign in February 1974 was intended to bring them a sympathy vote and had been detonated by a special unit for that purpose. Everyone believed it: the unionists, the nationalists, the Irish to the south, and many of those in Britain, even those who defended their army. Many believed that the British army had set up the killing of the IRSP political leaders after the INLA murdered Airey Neave on 31 March 1979.

Even more believed that the security forces had not only failed to protect republicans but had furnished the loyalists with targets and intelligence. Certainly the potential targets assumed that the Ulster Defence Regiment was filled with those friendly to the loyalist paramilitaries, were themselves in proven instances loyalist paramilitaries as well. The subsequent investigations, like that of Stalker, often attracted more attention as evidence surfaced of a continuing cover-up and so generated still more publicity.

Those who supported the security forces either did not believe the evidence or did not care, favoured a policy of shoot-to-kill or co-opting the loyalist gunmen. Such enthusiasm for pragmatic and successful covert operations was nowhere more easily found than in Westminster. Those who detested the Irish in general and the IRA in particular – no small population once the Provo bombs began going off in England – liked to assume that the dirty tricks were working. For a great many, Gibraltar was a success, greeted with enthusiasm rather than dismay.

As well as the increasing hard evidence of bodies scattered on the ground there were the revelations from inside the security forces. Books appeared, often issued in the midst of considerable controversy that engendered still more publicity and further accusations. Each of the authors gave a special inside perspective on the covert. Wright's *Spycatcher* gave an insight not so much into the details of dirty tricks in Ireland but rather into the limited and peculiarly myopic view of his colleagues: Harold Wilson was a red, and many "wets" in London were equally suspect, not aware of the needs of those in the field. Colin Wallace's and Fred Holroyd's books were discounted in part because of effective attacks on the credibility of the authors. Wallace had been accused and convicted of murder; Holroyd, who had been stashed in a mental hospital by the British army, had his stability and recollections regularly questioned in public forums without the opportunity to reply. Those who wanted to believe them did so, and those who did not did not. All these works were flawed, but all indicated the nature of the official toleration of intelligence adventures in disinformation, special operations and dirty tricks that could not be adequately discounted. More to the point, great effort was expended by someone in proving their revelations flawed, their stability doubtful.

Their evidence, like that of the critics, entered the analytical vernacular: the Littlejohns and other freelance agents; the adventures of Robert Nairac in south Armagh; the shoot-to-kill policy of the RUC and SAS; the intrusions across the border; the ambushes and tolerated murders; the disinformation coming out of British army headquarters at Lisburn; the special units that shifted name and location but not mission; the involvement of the security forces with the loyalists. All these dirty tricks were taken as given as the years passed. All were, therefore, indicators that there might be more to the Dublin bombs than an almost spontaneous loyalist incursion with limited rationalisation.

The British authorities, long possessed of high marks, often self-awarded, in intelligence matters – despite Philby and company – had certainly not produced a distinguished Irish record with their special operations. There were ludicrous failures, like the Littlejohn escapade or the rogue agents who, like Nairac, often brought disaster on themselves – singing rebel songs in a recently acquired Belfast accent in a pub in south

Armagh. And such operators brought also ignominy on their masters. There was the obvious hypocrisy that extended all the way up the judicial ladder from the arrest on the street or the use of the Prevention of Terrorism Act to harass anyone, any of the Irish, on through ploys like the coroner's inquest in Gibraltar. The failures of the British system culminated in the scandals surrounding the Irish bombing convictions and appeals. This tended to indicate that anything was possible, that the system was without shame.

Lord Denning defended the system over justice, in public and without qualms. Everywhere the system had been defended, the cover maintained, no matter how illogical or how great the cost. Secrets were secrets, and so in Ireland it was possible to believe anything. And some did.

Anything was indeed possible, except absolute proof; and so the system could evade responsibility or at least delay retribution. And this was true with the Dublin bombings of the early seventies: lots of circumstantial evidence, lots of details that could not be used in court, ample indicators and compelling logic, but never the tangibles needed in a court of law, by a disinterested historian, or by those who would otherwise be driven to respond officially to what remained speculation. In fact it was not until July 1993, when Yorkshire Television broadcast its investigation of the 1974 bombs, that the UVF took responsibility. Even then few could trust such spokesmen – not after twenty years of evasions and lies and when most of the suspects were long dead or in exile.

Not even then, after over two years' work by Yorkshire Television, was there a single shred of official evidence on British involvement in the 1974 bombs. And there had been nothing to add from inside the security forces, nothing from the supergrass trials, nothing really from Colin Wallace and Fred Holroyd, nothing tangible from anyone, only speculation. After twenty years no agent of the Crown, no soldier or constable, no official, no one had come forth to admit guilty knowledge, to admit anything. The UVF claimed to have been working alone, and the usable material released by the Gardaí to Yorkshire

Television could not carry the story further except by interpolation.

So the Dublin bombs had generated all sorts of compelling analysis and circumstantial evidence, often convincing data, but evidence that could not be used in court. The Garda Síochána's dictation from their book of evidence remains the bedrock of any speculation. All else is derived from projections and possibilities.

What the Yorkshire producers combined for an hour of compelling television was the reality of 1974, the evidence of the Gardaí, the record of the British security forces, the logic of the operation, and so a possible scenario. What they could not make was a certain case against the British security forces, and most certainly not a case that would require official British investigation. No one who mattered had talked, then or before. No new data could be taken alone as absolutely convincing.

The assumption that the incident was a military operation and that the UVF lacked the talent and capacity to act alone is still an assumption, not proof. Those who had long assumed that the loyalists were involved had the Garda data on the mid-Ulster UVF at one remove. Those who did not want to contemplate such matters did not. There, once more, the matter rested.

In the end the specifics of the bombing operations, the degree of involvement of the security forces in Northern Ireland and the precise bureaucratic fate of the investigation remain vague and unsatisfactory. In part this is obviously because all is not known, but in part all such operations remain vague. Doing nothing is hard to document. There is no evidence of a wink or a failure to ask. What is relevant – and remains so – is the public record that indicates the reality of the times, the ambiguity of the attitudes of those involved, and the reticence of all at the time and later to delve too deeply into matters that might only indicate past actions best neglected.

Someone planted the bombs in Dublin and Monaghan in 1972–74 and for both general and specific purpose. The chosen candidates have always been the loyalist paramilitaries, even if some wistfully hoped the IRA might have been responsible, at least for the December 1972 explosions. And in the case of May

1974 the specific involvement of the mid-Ulster UVF can be taken as actual, though not a matter of law. Far more interesting has been the almost universal assumption of most actors and nearly all observers in Ireland that the British in some manner were involved, certainly in 1972 and almost certainly in 1974, whether directly or indirectly, by rogue elements in the field or through special groups operating independently of higher command. The very fact that neither the RUC nor the British army undertook serious investigation is an indicator that the possibility was quite real north of the border, within the security establishment as well as in the Republic.

The British were then and are now considered by most people in Ireland guilty by association with the illegal loyalist paramilitaries, who have often been on their payroll, regularly considered their creatures. How could the UVF operate at such a level in 1974 without the authorities knowing – at least knowing afterwards? The UVF had always been carefully monitored, some bought and paid for, including at least two involved in the 1974 incident. Thus the British have been judged by the Irish public as guilty by implication, guilty out of arrogance, guilty on an operational level or carelessness further up the chain of command, but guilty. Jack Lynch said so for 1972. Yorkshire Television said so for 1974. In fact nearly everyone except those with obvious reasons to declare otherwise felt then and still feel that the British were involved somehow. There is almost but not quite evidence, almost but not quite a case made.

Many – not all – have come away from the chronicle of those bombs a generation ago with an abiding suspicion not simply of British propriety and innocence but also of the enormous risks of the covert and illicit deployed by the irresponsible for state purpose. Such adventures have been cloaked with a flag of patriotism and rationalised as pragmatism by other democracies. National security unleashed a French attack on the protest boat *Rainbow Warrior* in the Pacific, and the adventures of the American colonel Oliver North in Iran and Nicaragua were excused by pleading the needs of national security. National security for the pragmatic patriot seemingly permits murder as a policy option and shapes atrocity so that in the end no one is responsible, except those caught holding the smoking gun.

In Northern Ireland such matters of evasion and denial have become institutionalised. Since none can be found guilty, the observer is apt to assume that all are guilty. Those in London or the Northern Ireland Office who abhorred such deeds are also British and in responsible positions. Those who would never condone and who even oppose such acts often hold positions of trust under the Crown. Most important, an establishment's attitudes make the distant responsible as well. Even Soldier B learns of speeches made in Parliament about "swift justice" in Gibraltar or Armagh. Such attitudes about Irish matters led in no small way to the involvement of those whose careers flourished on the covert edge, for they acted not only as individuals but also as agents of the nation.

It is this assumption that "the British" are guilty in some degree that matters more than the details of the involvement. The accumulated evasion and hypocrisy on Irish matters has eroded faith in British integrity. This is, of course, especially true in Ireland, where British integrity and disinterest often wore thin. There is a reluctance on the part of much of the Dublin establishment to accept this judgement. To do so would largely ruin necessary and useful contact with those so involved, at no matter how many removes, with dirty tricks. As always, the British have given little thought to the dilemma of the Irish Government: let Dublin do as London wants, knows is best; let Dublin get on with what is needed and give up whingeing. And all Dublin wants is a little British discretion: no more dirty tricks, or at least no more revelations of dirty tricks.

The assumption within the London establishment has always been that propriety, honour, justice and common decency are a special local specie coined over time by a grand tradition that would not be frittered away in the unsavoury aspects of war and politics. In Ireland, not unexpectedly, the assumptions of the British have long been sold at discount. This is especially so because British spokesmen regularly seem not so much content as delighted with many of the dirty tricks. The authorities were often so determined to support their own in the field that they in fact only recognised the validity of criticism by recourse to cover-up at great cost. Thus in London it was assumed that no honour was lost. If honour is lost it is because it is perceived to be lost; and unconventional wars, dirty wars, are focused on perceptions, not tangibles. arrect

Neither the IRA-loyalist ceasefires nor the uncertain peace process that has eroded the need for special operations and intrusive intelligence can easily allow the British to regain the assets of legitimacy and civility damaged during the Troubles. The costs are not swiftly recouped – suspicions are long-lived, presumptions of guilty not readily discarded. Long after the details of the Dublin bombs are forgotten the residue of general and particular distaste will remain: decency lost swiftly regained.

In the end the murders in the street, the grief and horror, arose from the corruption of the unionist tradition and, more important, from the nature of the British involved with the Irish Troubles. Some who came to Ireland were decent, some not, but all to some degree became engaged in a nasty, brutal campaign in an arena that was alien. And these, the responsible, operated in the name of virtues often long lost, often corrupted, too often inapplicable in Ireland. Those who in dubious battle seek recourse to terror, to murder the monster, may find themselves judged monster, fairly or not – for there is little justice in a dirty war, in the waging of battles in violation of the ideals of the nation, ideals long in the winning and easily lost, and long lost for many in Ireland.

Sources

There are no conventional sources for the Dublin bombs, not even any very useful speculative or secondary sources. The governments involved, like all governments when concerned with national security matters, special operations, or intelligence, especially when such matters have contemporary political consequences, are inevitably mute. Even when the facts in such cases are public and patent, governments prefer to deny comment or to deny reality if need be – even after generations, in the more sensitive cases. The operational individuals involved in all the bomb cases have said nothing, even after a generation, either in public or in private, that has had more general currency.

For a generation no one has said anything, except for the Gardaí. The individuals within the Gardaí who have commented did so for a special purpose, now served, and, as they indicated for example in August 1993, have no interest in elaboration. Even now some of the Garda information remains with Yorkshire Television, unbroadcast, too sensitive for various reasons to make public. So there can be no official sources, no individuals directly concerned who might be forthcoming, only the speculative and conventional.

Most of those concerned with special operations and dirty tricks have focused on Northern Ireland and on events there, not in Dublin or Monaghan; even the Nairac intrusions are shaped to a Northern arena. Thus Mark Urban's *Big Boys' Rules: the Secret Struggle against the IRA* on one side and those works more critical of the security forces – for example Patsy McArdle, *The Secret War*, Martin Dillon, *The Dirty War*, Anthony Bradley, *Requiem for a Spy: the Killing of Robert Nairac*, and Mícheál Ó Cuinneagáin, *The Nairac Affair* – are not concerned with the bombs except in passing.

Those works by Dillon and others, and especially Steven Bruce's *The Red Hand: Protestant Paramilitaries in Northern Ireland,* add nothing new on the bombs. Bruce simply notes in passing that the 1974 bombings, for example, were probably by the loyalist paramilitaries. Any of the various works on the "supergrass" trials and especially on the Stalker affair – John Stalker, *Stalker*, and Peter Taylor, *Stalker: the Search for the Truth* – indicate the investment the British government will make in seeing that special operations remain special and secret, just as the Gibraltar case was to prove once again.

Those who do seek to reveal the nature of British intelligence at play in Ireland treat the bombs, if at all, as an aside, for example Peter Wright, *Spycatcher*, Fred Holroyd, *War Without Honour*, and Paul Foot, *Who Framed Colin Wallace?* The material arising from these revelations – usually found in the newspapers and reviews of the times – merely adds to the general rather than particular knowledge

The views of the Dublin establishment are best found at some length in Garret FitzGerald's *All in a Life: an Autobiography*, which offers nothing novel on the bombs, as was the case with those who commented on the Yorkshire Television programme, the consensus being that those in the Government knew nothing and most of those involved had doubts about any British involvement. Those who did assume such an involvement rested their case not on sources but on assumptions and speculations that fall outside conventional sources. The plain tale is to be found in the newspapers of the day, in the Garda revelations, in the limited comments of the involved; and this clearly leaves more than adequate room for conspiracy theories and logical projects – speculation.

References

Anthony Bradley, *Requiem for a Spy: the Killing of Robert Nairac* (Mercier, Cork and Dublin, 1993).

Steven Bruce, *The Red Hand: Protestant Paramilitaries in Northern Ireland* (Oxford University Press, Oxford, 1992).

Martin Dillon, *The Dirty War* (Hutchinson, London, 1990).

Garret FitzGerald, *All in a Life: an Autobiography* (Gill & Macmillan, Dublin, 1991).

Paul Foot, *Who Framed Colin Wallace?* (Macmillan, London, 1989).

Fred Holroyd with Nick Burbridge, *War Without Honour* (Medium, Hull, 1989).

Patsy McArdle, *The Secret War* (Mercier, Cork, 1984).

Raymond Murray, *The SAS in Ireland* (Mercier, Cork and Dublin, 1990).

Micheál Ó Cuinneagáin, *The Nairac Affair* (Tanatallon, Donegal, 1981).

John Stalker, *Stalker* (Harrap, London, 1988).

Peter Taylor, *Stalker: the Search for the Truth* (Faber and Faber, London, 1987).

Mark Urban, *Big Boys' Rules: the Secret Struggle against the IRA* (Faber and Faber, London, 1992).

Peter Wright with Paul Greengrass, *Spycatcher* (Viking, London, 1987).